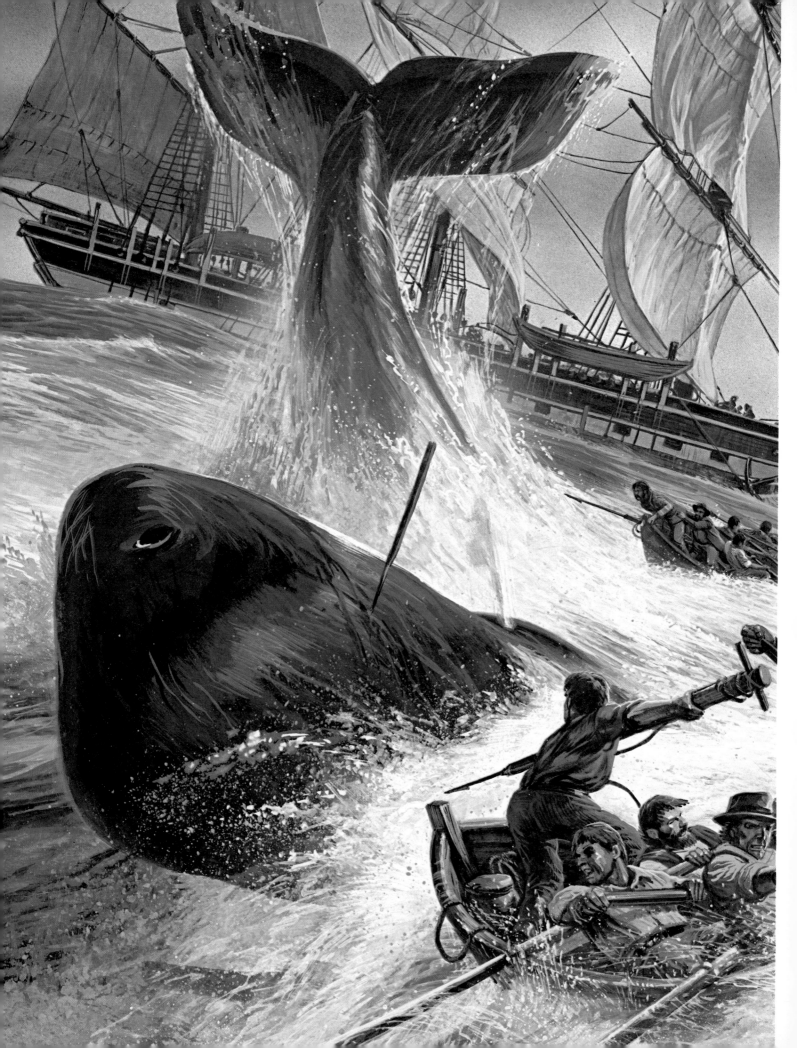

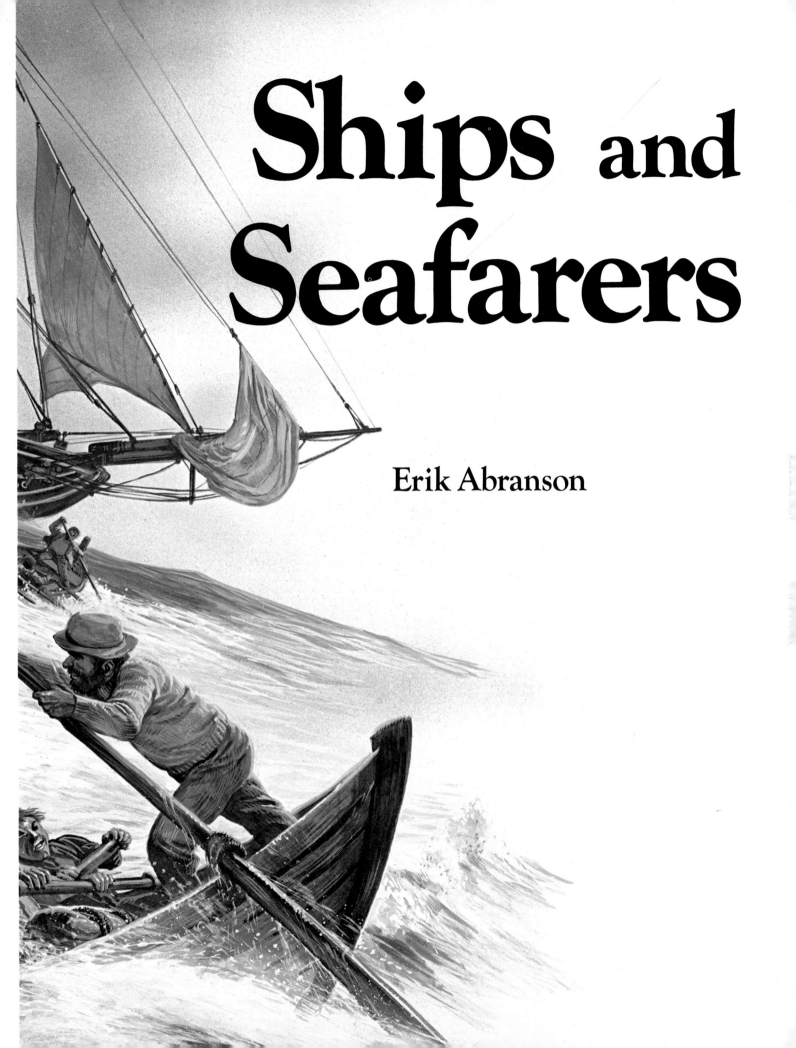

Ships and
Seafarers

Erik Abranson

First published in 1979 by
Macdonald Educational Ltd
Holywell House
Worship Street
London EC2A 2EN

© Macdonald Educational 1979

ISBN 0-382-06382-1
Published in the
United States by
Silver Burdett
Company, Morristown, N.J.
1980 Printing
Library of Congress
Catalog Card No. 80-50953

Contents

Ships and seafarers of antiquity

No one knows when man first straddled a log to float on water but we do know that seafarers existed a long time before the first farmers because artifacts from pre-agricultural times have been found on many islands. The oldest known representations of boats are more than 5000 years old and have been found in Mesopotamia and in Egypt. They show reed boats of the type which still exist on Lake Titicaca (Peru); skin boats similar to present day Irish and Welsh coracles and Eskimo kayaks, and wooden ships.

The ancient Egyptian boatmen were by no means just river boatmen. They sailed all the way to the Lebanon and down the Red Sea to the land of Punt, which was probably Somalia. In 1850 BC they dug a canal which permitted vessels to sail from the Nile to the Red Sea. In this way they succeeded in linking the Red Sea to the Mediterranean more than 37 centuries before the opening of the Suez Canal!

The Minoans of Crete formed the first maritime empire which flourished from the 3rd millenium BC until 1470 BC when an eruption and explosion of the volcano on Thera island swept the Cretan harbours. A huge tidal wave buried the Cretan fields under thick layers of sterile ash. Some people think that the legend of the lost city of Atlantis referred to this advanced civilization which was enriched by its sea trade throughout the eastern Mediterranean.

The Greeks succeeded the Minoans as the major Mediterranean seafarers and founded many trading posts. It was from Massilia (Marseilles) that the astronomer and mathematician, Pytheas, set off in 325 BC to sail round Britain, to sail up to the Arctic ice-pack beyond Iceland and perhaps to explore the Baltic.

The Phoenicians were another important seafaring nation. In the 10th century BC their ships carried the cedar timbers to build Solomon's Temple and brought him the ivory and gems of Ophir, on the south Arabian coast. In 600 BC some Phoenicians sailed round Africa in three years. One hundred years later Hanno, from Carthage, led an expedition of 60 galleys and 30,000 men to colonize West Africa and pushed as far as Gabon. The Carthaginians were crushed by the Romans who eventually controlled all the sea trade from Egypt to Britain and Holland.

▲ This model is of a 400-year-old wooden Egyptian Nile boat. The shape of its curved hull and stern clearly shows its close relationship to the earlier papyrus-reed boat.

The butt ends of the beams protrude through the hull.

◄ The ancient Greek ships are mainly known to us through representations on pottery. Here is a naval galley, long and narrow for speed. The broader merchant vessel (left) usually relied on wind for propulsion.

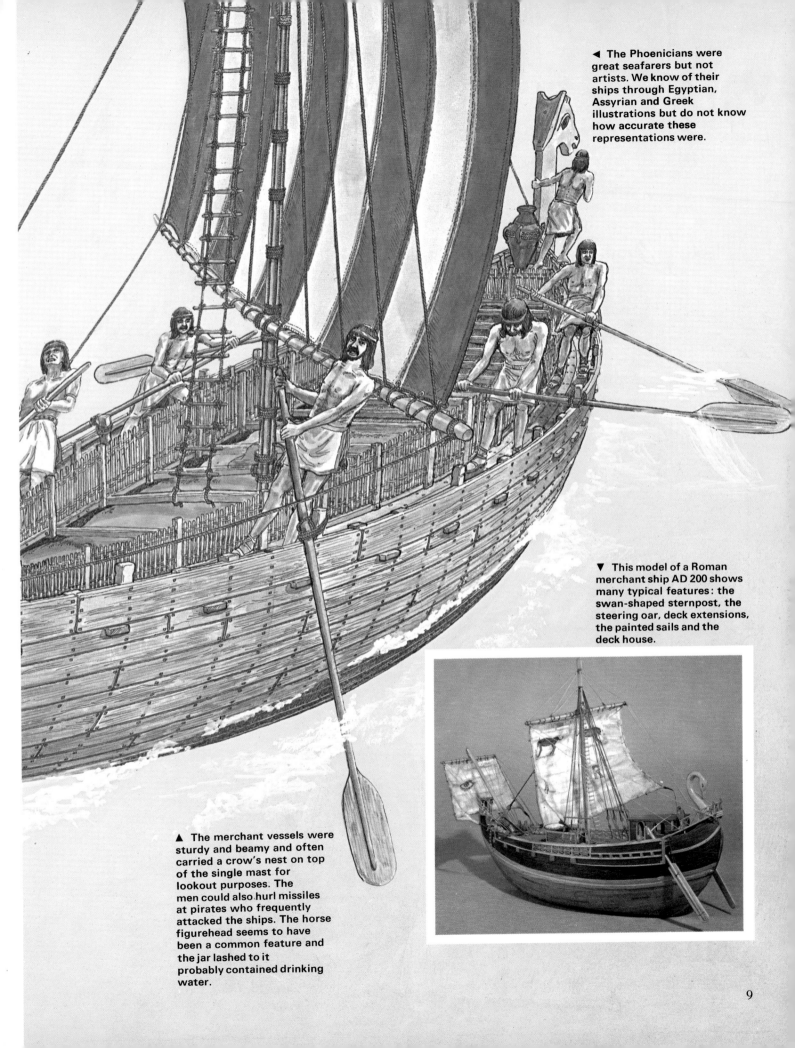

◄ The Phoenicians were great seafarers but not artists. We know of their ships through Egyptian, Assyrian and Greek illustrations but do not know how accurate these representations were.

▼ This model of a Roman merchant ship AD 200 shows many typical features: the swan-shaped sternpost, the steering oar, deck extensions, the painted sails and the deck house.

▲ The merchant vessels were sturdy and beamy and often carried a crow's nest on top of the single mast for lookout purposes. The men could also hurl missiles at pirates who frequently attacked the ships. The horse figurehead seems to have been a common feature and the jar lashed to it probably contained drinking water.

The Viking saga

'The Vikings are coming' was a cry that caused terror and panic in the coastal and riverside populations of the British Isles, the Low Countries and France in the latter years of the 8th century and in the 9th century AD. These were the years when the Christian populations were being raided and their villages looted by bands of fierce pagans from the North. The invaders came in fleets of longships powered by oars and a single large square sail.

In the following century the Vikings conquered lands and established their rule in the Highlands and Islands of Scotland, the Isle of Man, Ireland, and the North of England and in northern France (Normandy), where they eventually became Christians. They mixed with the native Celts, Saxons and Franks, who in turn adopted a number of Viking customs, some of which survive to the present day.

The voyages of the Vikings were not restricted to northwestern Europe. Their raids took them as far as Spain and to the entrance of the Mediterranean where they made contact with the Moors. In AD 860 they 'discovered' Iceland which had been thinly settled since the 6th century by Irish monks, and ten years later they started colonizing the island.

▼ The Vikings built many types of ships for war or commerce but they were all constructed with their planks overlapping (clinker-built) and all had raised ends.

The warships were in fact oared troop transports as the fighting was mainly done on land, and seldom at sea. The dragon figure-heads were carried on war cruises.

The Viking Explorations

GREENLAND
ICELAND
ATLANTIC OCEAN
Oslo
Birka
DENMARK
London
RUSSIA
Bulgar
GERMANY
Kiev
FRANCE
SPAIN
ITALY
BLACK SEA
CASPIAN SEA
GREECE
Constantinople
NORTH AFRICA
MEDITERRANEAN SEA
Bagdad

▲ The Vikings sailed far and wide from their Scandinavian homeland. They reached Iceland, Greenland and America in the west. To the east they travelled to Spain, Russia, the Caspian Sea and the Black Sea.

In 930 an Icelandic Viking was blown out to sea by a storm and sighted a new land. Fifty years later, a Norwegian Viking outcast, Erik the Red, sought refuge on this land. He called it Greenland and founded a colony there. One of his followers on his way from Iceland missed Greenland and sighted further islands to the west. These were investigated by Erik the Red's son, Leif Erikson, in AD 1000. He called them Helluland (Baffin Island), Markland (Labrador) and Vinland (Newfoundland and perhaps south to New England). His brother returned there a few years later only to be kidnapped by the Indians. A colonization attempt in 1020, led by the Icelander Thorfin Karlsefni, failed because of Indian attacks but the Vikings continued to trade occasionally in North America for furs until at least 1347.

Other Vikings, mainly Swedes, crossed the Baltic and traded along the Russian rivers in ships similar to those used on the ocean. Thus they reached the Caspian Sea and the Black Sea where they made contact with the Arabs and the Byzantines. These Vikings were called Rus and gave their name to Russia.

The Vikings ships are well known because they are depicted on many objects made by Vikings and non-Vikings alike. It was a Viking custom to bury (and sometimes burn) their chiefs in their ships. Several ships preserved by burial have been excavated, notably the Oseberg and Gokstad ships which are now on display in Oslo. They were all double-ended (pointed at both ends) and clinker-built (with their planks overlapping like shingles). The longships were the big warships, with 20 to 60 pairs of oars and sometimes almost 180 metres long. The Vikings also used similar but smaller ships for war and trade, coastal vessels and beamy cargo vessels.

Medieval shipping

Many important technological changes in the field of shipping appeared during the Middle Ages. From the earliest times steering had been done by means of oars lashed to the side of the ship near the stern; on big ships such oars were unwieldy and inefficient. Early in the 13th century the modern stern rudder appeared in northwestern Europe. It had been known in China since the 1st century AD. If the European invention came from China, how it happened remains a mystery.

The magnetic compass was another 1st century Chinese invention; it appeared in Italy in the 13th century. This can be explained by contact with Arabs who in turn had contact with Chinese junks in the Indian Ocean. The use of the rudder and the compass allowed a more precise course to be steered, making deep-sea passages less hazardous. The third major innovation was the fore-and-aft rig, the lateen (triangular) sail which superseded the square sail in the Mediterranean sometime between the 3rd and 10th centuries. Such a sail made it possible for ships to be sailed to windward.

From the 12th century some German towns such as Lübeck, Hamburg and Bremen formed a trading association known as the Hanseatic League. This league traded throughout the North Sea and the Baltic, carrying Baltic salted herring, Swedish copper and iron, German silver, salt, cloth and wool. For this trade, the cog, was evolved. This flat-bottomed, double ended vessel was convenient for bulky cargoes and well suited to North Sea conditions.

◀ Since prehistoric times steering had been achieved by one or more steering oars lashed onto the ship's side. This was given the name 'steerboard' later called starboard, a term which is still used today.

▶ The idea to hinge a rudder on the sternpost was a major technological invention which was made possible by the change from the curved sterns of early ships to the straight sterns of 12th and 13th century ships.

Around the Mediterranean Sea a number of City-States, especially Venice and Genoa, had a flourishing sea trade, importing silks and spices from Byzantium and Alexandria and exporting woven materials, glass-ware and slaves. They used short, beamy vessels with up to three decks for bulky or cheap cargoes, and sleek galleys for perishable or expensive cargoes. They eventually copied the cog, rigging it with lateen sails. The cog gradually changed into the bigger and more rounded carrack which in turn acquired more masts with several sails each, combining the square and the lateen rigs.

▲ The carrack first evolved in the Mediterranean as a two-masted vessel. By the days of Henry VIII it could have up to four **masts**, each setting several **sails**.

▲ The cog was the typical medieval North Sea ship and was the 'workhorse' of the Hanseatic League traders. The wooden battlements were removable and fitted only for passages where attack was feared.

◄ The Bayeux tapestry depicts the conquest of England in 1066 by the Normans who were the descendants of Vikings recently established in France. Their ships were similar to Viking longships. They often had linen sails of different colours which were sometimes embroidered in silk.

► This miniature from the *Chroniques de Froissart* depicts the Franco-British battle of l'Ecluse (1340).

Age of discoveries

The considerable progress in nautical craftsmanship which occured in late medieval times coincided with a deepening of the antagonism between Christians and Muslims in the 15th century. Because of their powerful geographical position, the Muslims had control over all trade to and from the Far East. Now they were taking advantage of their monopoly by increasing tolls and profits with traders. Christian missionary zeal was growing along with a renewed interest in the idea that the earth was round and that the Indies could be reached either by sailing round Africa or by sailing due west. All these factors together with a shortage of gold to aid the expansion of trade and industry, led to the great wave of maritime expansion and colonial conquest known as the 'Age of Discovery' in the late 15th and early 16th centuries.

The Portuguese had been sending a series of expeditions down the African coast, each reaching further south, until in 1488 Bartholomew Diaz sailed round the tip of South Africa. He discovered the 'Cape of Storms' which was renamed the 'Cape of Good Hope' upon his return because it was seen as the gateway to India. Diaz' expedition sailed in two 50-ton caravels.

Using the successful Portugese expedition to the South as an argument, Christopher Columbus, a Genoese seaman-adventurer, persuaded Ferdinand and Isabella of Castille to let him find the direct western route to the Indies. He sailed in 1492 with three ships, the *Santa Maria*, the *Nina*, and the *Pinta*. The *Santa Maria* was a nao (small carrack) and the other two were smaller caravels. From the Canary Islands it took Columbus 38 days of sailing unknown seas to reach land. He arrived at Watling Island in the Bahamas—which he mistakenly took to be Japan. He has also been acclaimed as the discoverer of America but he was preceded in the 6th century by Irish Monks, by 10th century Vikings and, in his own days, by Basque, Breton and Dieppe fishermen who were already fishing the Newfoundland banks and salting cod ashore. Columbus did however discover the West Indies before sailing home.

On his second voyage Columbus discovered other Caribbean islands and he actually set foot on the American mainland on his third voyage (1498). It was on his fourth and last voyage that he finally realized that he was nowhere near Cipango and Cathay (Japan and China).

In 1497–99 the Portuguese explorer Vasco da Gama discovered the practical route to India by way of the Cape of Good Hope. His expedition consisted of two naos, a caravel and a storeship. The Pacific was first sighted, from Panama, in 1513. The great expedition which completed this golden age of exploration was the first round-the-world voyage achieved in 1519–22 by Ferdinand Magellan's men—Magellan himself being killed on the way.

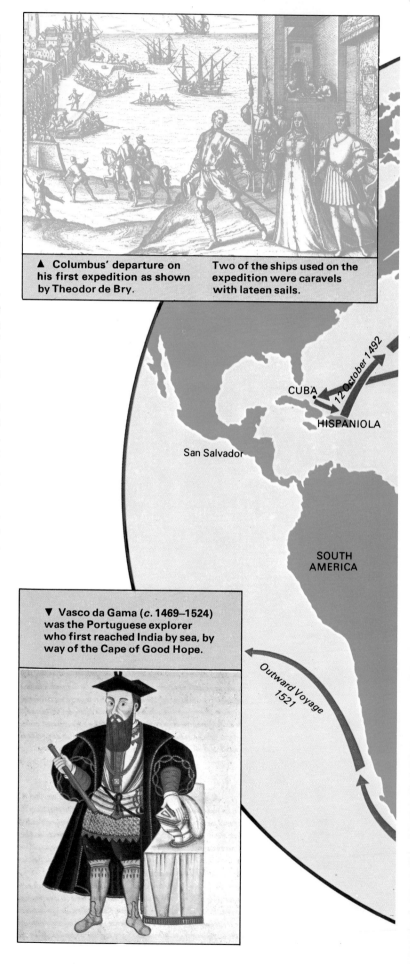

▲ Columbus' departure on his first expedition as shown by Theodor de Bry.

Two of the ships used on the expedition were caravels with lateen sails.

CUBA

HISPANIOLA

San Salvador

12 October 1492

SOUTH AMERICA

▼ Vasco da Gama (*c.* 1469–1524) was the Portuguese explorer who first reached India by sea, by way of the Cape of Good Hope.

Outward Voyage 1521

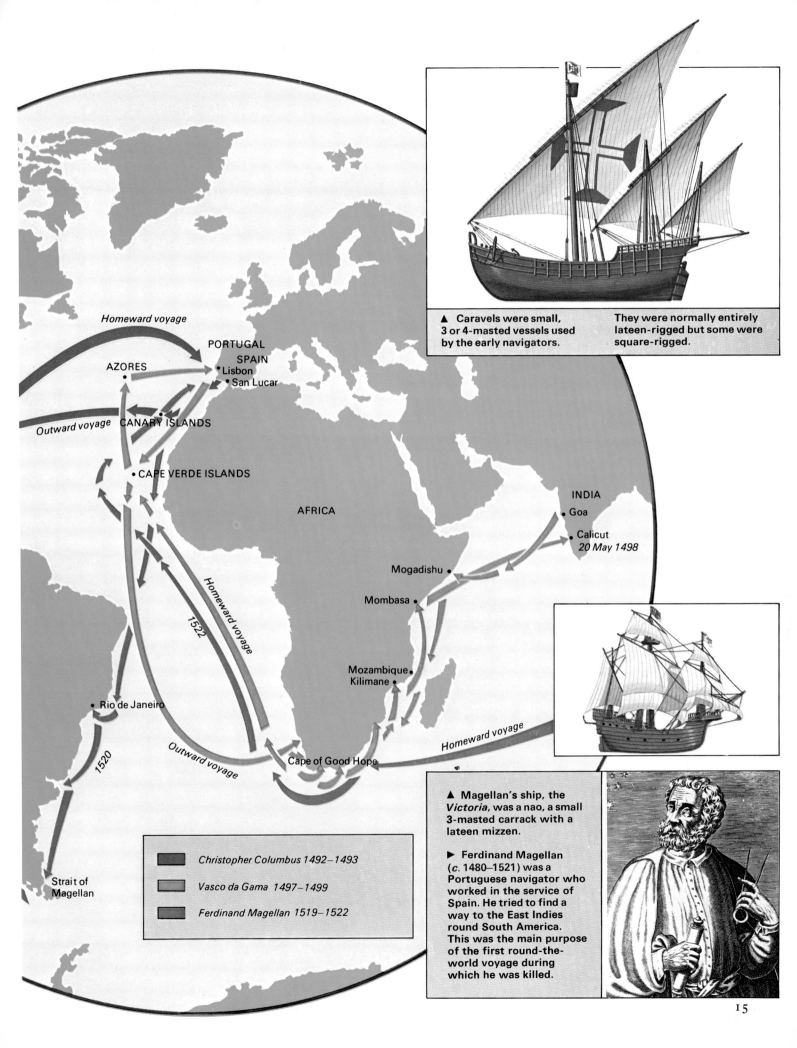

Homeward voyage

PORTUGAL
SPAIN
AZORES
• Lisbon
• San Lucar

Outward voyage   CANARY ISLANDS

• CAPE VERDE ISLANDS

AFRICA

INDIA
• Goa
• Calicut
20 May 1498

Mogadishu •

Mombasa •

1522

Homeward voyage

Mozambique •
Kilimane •

• Rio de Janeiro

1520

Outward voyage   Cape of Good Hope   Homeward voyage

Strait of
Magellan

	Christopher Columbus 1492–1493
	Vasco da Gama 1497–1499
	Ferdinand Magellan 1519–1522

▲ Caravels were small,
3 or 4-masted vessels used
by the early navigators.

They were normally entirely
lateen-rigged but some were
square-rigged.

▲ Magellan's ship, the
Victoria, was a nao, a small
3-masted carrack with a
lateen mizzen.

► Ferdinand Magellan
(*c.* 1480–1521) was a
Portuguese navigator who
worked in the service of
Spain. He tried to find a
way to the East Indies
round South America. This
was the main purpose
of the first round-the-
world voyage during
which he was killed.

The galleys

Galleys usually had one or more auxiliary sails although, of course, they were primarily intended to be rowed. The use of oars meant that the ship needed to have a narrow beam and a comparatively great length. During its 3,000 year history, the galley changed remarkably little in its appearance. Galleys were expensive to man (even with slave oarsmen) and were seldom used as merchant ships except for light, expensive or perishable cargoes. Their freedom from reliance on the wind made them useful as fighting ships. They were, however, unseaworthy in open ocean conditions and they were used mainly in the Mediterranean Sea.

The earliest known picture of a sea battle is an 1190 BC relief on an Egyptian temple, which shows the victorious engagement of the galleys of Rameses II against the 'Sea People'. The other seafaring nations of the ancient Mediterranean also used galleys, notably the Greeks who had galleys with two levels or 'banks' of oars (biremes) or three (triremes). In 480 BC Greece was being overrun by the Persians and the Greeks mustered their fleet of 335 triremes in the Strait of Salamis. In these confined waters the much larger Persian fleet could not be used efficiently so the Greeks were able to sink 200 Persian galleys and captured many others. The Battle of Salamis, the most decisive of all naval history, saved Greece from Persian rule. Later Greek galleys had four, five and up to 40 banks of oars—this means that there were still only three levels of oars, but each cluster of three oars was manned by four to 40 rowers. Some galleys were armed to resist rams and the bolts and boulders hurled by catapults.

The 12th century Byzantines replaced the unwieldy three-banked galleys by the fast double-banked dromon, which had up to 200 rowers and was fitted with a flame thrower (Greek fire) in the bows. The 15th century Venetians invented the 'modern' galley with a single bank of long, heavy sweeps pulled by five men each.

The last important galley battle was that of Lepanto in 1571 where 200 galleys of the Holy League destroyed all but 40 galleys of a 250-strong Turkish fleet. By then the appearance of the broadside artillery of sailing ships was already spelling the end of the galleys; it was impossible to fit more than five guns in the bows of the galleys and they only fired straight ahead.

▶ The last great galley battle was that of Lepanto in 1571 where galleys and galleasses of the Holy League (mainly Venetian and Spanish) defeated the Turks. The Venetian ensigns show the Lion of St. Mark and the Turkish ones bear crescents.

▼ A model of a Greek trireme of c. 500 BC. It was rowed at three levels with one man to each oar. There were usually 170 rowers who rowed in time to a flautist.

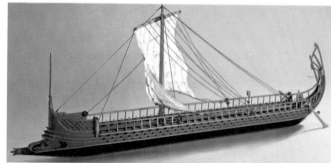

In 1684 the French warship *Le Bon* smashed an entire fleet of 35 galleys. The great French galley fleet (with up to seven men per oar) operating between 1643 and 1715 was not a fighting fleet but a symbol of prestige and a method of punishment.

A few galleys were kept by minor Mediterranean powers. The last naval battle in which galleys were actively used was at Matapan (southern Greece) in 1717. The English, Swedes and Russians used galleys in the 17th and early 18th centuries but without much success. Galleys were gradually phased out because they were no match against the men-o'-war.

▶ An artist's impression of oarsmen rowing a Turkish galley. During the 16th century galleys were often rowed by as many as five men to each oar. Greater speed was achieved by using fewer oars and increasing the number of men pulling on each oar.

▲ Turkish galleys of *c*. 1636 attacking small Christian craft. Notice the single bank of oars and the forward firing guns.

Spanish gold: Francis Drake

Francis Drake was a controversial character. For the English he was a national hero, as well as a great privateer who successfully challenged the unjust monopolistic power of the Spaniards. He was knighted by Queen Elizabeth for his adventures. For the Spaniards, he was a villainous English pirate. Pirate or privateer, he was a first class seaman whose adventurous life is typical of the rip-roaring spirit of Elizabethan England.

▼ Francis Drake (c. 1541–1596) in his 39th year, just after the return from his circumnavigation, which netted £500,000 profit and gained him a knighthood. He was a great navigator and sea commander and was extremely well-liked by his sailors.

▲ Elizabeth I (1533–1603) was the arch-enemy of Spain because of religious and economic interests. She was Drake's patron and had a share in the profits of his slaving and privateering expeditions.

▼ In 1579 Drake landed on the North American Pacific coast in a place he called Nova Albion. He was well received by the natives, and stopped to refit his ships there.

▼ The *Golden Hind*, a replica of the famous galleon that took Drake round the world. This replica was built at Appledore, Devon in 1975 and sailed to San Francisco where she is now a tourist attraction.

▶ Drake's brilliant attack on Cadiz harbour in 1587 is explained on this map signed by Vice Admiral Borough. The action became known as 'the singeing of the King of Spain's beard' and prevented the Armada from sailing that year

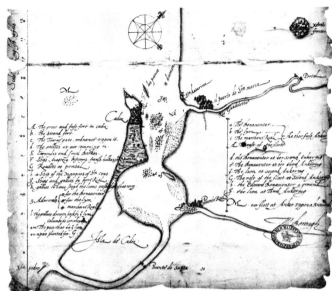

He was 28 years old when he sailed on his first long voyage. The first leg of the journey was to Africa to buy or capture some slaves. The second leg was to the Spanish West Indies to sell the cargo illegally as the Spanish forbade any foreign ships to trade with her possessions. Where the local Spaniards refused to trade, armed action would follow. In Mexico the Spanish sunk a couple of the English ships and Drake barely escaped with his life. This adventure gave him the hearty loathing of the Spaniards which motivated his later career, in particular his voyage round the world in 1577–80, then only the second circumnavigation ever done.

The expedition started from Plymouth with five ships. Drake sailed in a small galleon, the *Pelican*, which he later renamed *Golden Hind*. After stops at the Cape Verde Islands, Brazil and Argentina, he went through the Strait of Magellan in a fast 17 days. Later he was blown south and east by a terrific storm which landed him on Horn Island—leading him to discover the Cape Horn passage. Drake then sailed into the Pacific and plundered the unprotected Spanish settlements of the west coast of South America, finally capturing the richest prize ship of all, the *Nuestra Senora de la Concepción*. She was laden with 360,000 gold coins plus silver bars and coins. He finally returned home by sailing west, stopping at Ternate (Indonesia) to load a valuable cargo of cloves from under the noses of the Portuguese.

Spain retaliated against these outrages by seizing English ships. In return Drake led an expedition of 22 ships and 2300 men in 1585–86. He burned Santiago in the Cape Verde Islands, looted Santo Domingo and Cartagena (in Columbia) and destroyed St Augustine in Florida. In 1587 he destroyed 24 vessels in Cadiz harbour and captured the Portuguese East-India carrack *São Felipe*. In 1588 he was one of the Armada heroes but his last two expeditions were both failures. He died from fever in 1596.

The Great Armada

King Philip II of Spain and Portugal was so incensed at the continuing attacks by the English against his ships that he decided to teach them a lesson by invading England. He mustered a large army under the command of the Duke of Parma in Flanders. In order to cover the ferrying of the army in barges across the Dover Strait, Philip assembled the largest fleet the world had ever seen, the Great Armada. Its commander, the Duke of Medina Sidonia, was a soldier whose nobility did not make up for his lack of experience at sea.

The Armada consisted of 130 ships from Spain, Portugal and Italy. It included ponderous and power-fully armed galleons, galleasses, galleys, armed mer-chantmen and storeships.

Waiting for this fleet at Plymouth the English had 64 ships, under the command of Lord Howard of Effingham. Twenty-four of these were English galleons which did not carry the clumsy superstructures of the Spanish galleons.

After many delays and setbacks the Armada sailed out of Corunna and was sighted off the Lizard, Cornwall, on 29 June 1588. Despite an adverse wind the English fleet sailed out of Plymouth and got to a commanding position windward of the Armada. At close range the Spaniards had the advantage of heavier guns and more men, so the English fought at a distance with their superior longe-range gunnery. This created a confusion in which two Spanish ships collided and the disabled one fell back to be picked up by one of Drake's galleons. Another Spanish ship blew up in mysterious circumstances. The fight drifted up Channel, with considerable waste of ammunition, but the English were being resupplied from the shore whereas the Spaniards were running short.

▶ The Armada's failure to land in England turned into disaster when it had to flee round Scotland and Ireland.

◀ The battle of Plymouth showing the small English Western Fleet attacking the Armada which is sailing in crescent formation. The later capture of the *Rosario* by the *Revenge* is shown on the lower left.

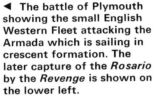

▶ Detail of a painting showing one of the galleons of the Spanish Armada sinking.

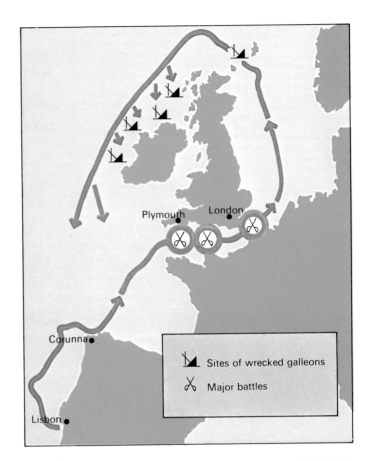

Plymouth • London

Corunna •

⚓ Sites of wrecked galleons

✂ Major battles

Lisbon •

Meanwhile Parma's landing barge fleet was being effectively blockaded by the Dutch Protestants, who were collaborating with the English. The Armada could not go in to relieve the barges because the water was too shallow for its ships, so it anchored at Calais on 7 August 1588, to await events. That night the English sent eight fireships into Calais which created a massive panic; most of the Spanish ships cut their anchor cables to escape. The ships fled north where they were hounded by the English fleet. With a continuing south-west wind and a shortage of ammunition, the scattered Armada ships could not face the English again by going back through the Channel. They had no choice but to sail into the North Sea, round Scotland and past Ireland. Many men died of starvation. Great storms also wrecked many of the ships causing no fewer than 20 to be lost on the Irish coast. Only 80 vessels limped back to Spain, most of them beyond repair and with depleted crews. The 'invincible' Armada had received a crushing defeat and Spain had lost her maritime supremacy.

The Dutch Wars

In the 17th century one out of every five Dutchmen was a sailor or a fisherman and in 1650 nine-tenths of all cargoes landed or loaded in English harbours were carried by Dutch ships. To protect the declining English merchant shipping Oliver Cromwell passed the Navigation Act in 1651, which forbade foreign ships to load or land cargoes in England which were not going to or coming from the country of the carrier. This move was of course aimed at the Dutch ships and was a disastrous blow for Dutch commerce, making war inevitable.

The First Dutch War started in 1652. The Dutch admiral Maarten Tromp with 40 ships, met the English 'general-at-sea' Robert Blake in the Channel. Blake had 12 warships which were joined during the battle by nine others. Despite the difference in numbers Blake captured two Dutch ships but his own ship, the *James*, and many other English ships received a battering. Blake then sailed into the North Sea where he destroyed the Dutch herring fishing fleet.

Sailing in winter, when half the English fleet were laid up, Tromp defeated the English ships sent to intercept a Dutch merchant convoy of 500 sail. He sailed back to Holland with a broom at his masthead, to show that he had swept the English from the seas! He was crying victory too soon, however, for five Dutch vessels were caught or sunk by Blake and George Monck in a three-day battle early in 1653. Tromp was killed at the decisive battle on 11 June off the North Foreland (Kent) where the Dutch lost 10 of their 90 vessels to the English fleet of 110 sail. Peace was signed in 1654 but did not really solve the problem of Anglo-Dutch rivalry at sea.

The Second Dutch War erupted in 1665. In June the Duke of York won the battle of Lowestoft, where the Dutch admiral Obdam was killed in the explosion of his flagship. A year later, the Dutch admiral Michiel de Ruyter won the Four Days' Battle against Monck. Monck got his own back later at the St James Day Battle off North Foreland and later burnt down a Dutch harbour. In 1667 de Ruyter managed to enter the Thames estuary with his fleet and captured and burned many ships. This was a great humiliation for the English but happened too late to change the course of war. An inconclusive peace was signed.

Five years later the Third Dutch War was declared, with France and England allied against the Dutch. Threatened by the biggest sea power and the biggest land power, Holland would have been lost without the strategic genius of de Ruyter. As it was, the three big battles of Sole Bay in 1672 and of Schoneveldt and Texel in 1673 had no outright victors and England withdrew from the alliance. The English claimed they had been let down by the French, who later won an inconclusive victory over the Dutch fleet in 1676, leaving England as the major sea power.

◄ George Monck (1608–70), a soldier by training, was made a 'General at Sea' by Cromwell and he became a talented admiral. He supported the Restoration and was made Duke of Albemarle.

▼ Dutch merchantmen at Amsterdam in 1620. In the 17th century Dutch shipping dominated world trade and the three Anglo-Dutch wars were largely due to England's challenge to Dutch supremacy.

◀ The Four Days' Battle (June 1–4 1666) painted by William Van de Velde. In this drawn-out battle off Dunkirk, de Ruyter defeated Monck and Prince Rupert.

▲ Maarten Tromp (1597–1653) was a formidable opponent of the English.

▶ Michiel Adrianszoon de Ruyter (1607–76) was a brilliant Dutch admiral who fought in all three Anglo-Dutch wars. He was described as 'a man worth an army' and was mourned even by his enemies.

The skull and crossbones

Pirates and Buccaneers! These names conjure up ideas of high adventure, excitement and buried treasure—but piracy is nothing more than banditry at sea and in reality the cry of 'Pirates!' would be more likely to bring shivers of fear than a thrill of excitement. Piracy is as old as seafaring—a form of it still exists today—but its heyday was between the 16th and 18th centuries.

The Barbarossa brothers Arouj and Kheir-ed-Din were two of the famous Barbary (North Africa) pirates. They lived around AD 1600. Arouj gained fame by capturing, with a much smaller galliot, two galleys belonging to the Pope, just off the coast of Italy. However he murdered almost as many Muslims as Christians and he was finally assassinated by his own followers. His brother Kheir-ed-Din had a more successful career and died a rich man in old age, an unusual fate for a pirate.

Monbars the 'Exterminator' and L'Olonois were two notorious and blood-thirsty French buccaneers of the 17th century who made a speciality of looting and murdering Spaniards in the Caribbean. L'Olonois, who had once eaten the heart of a Spaniard, later was killed and eaten by Carib natives.

Henry Morgan was undoubtedly the king of the free-booters in the mid 17th century. He ransacked Cuba, took Porto Bello (Panama) and pillaged the town of Panama. The booty included 200 mule loads of gold coins. He was arrested and sent back to England to face trial, but instead was knighted by Charles II and returned to Jamaica . . . as governor and in charge of repressing piracy, a task which he fulfilled quite effectively!

'Blackbeard' Edward Teach was a colossal and colourful pirate operating along the American east coast in the 18th century. He sported a huge beard which he plaited with ribbons. He carried a sash across his chest with three braces of pistols and in his hat he stuck a smouldering slowmatch (to ignite explosives).

There were also some women pirates. In the 18th century Anne Bonny, the daughter of a wealthy family, ran away from home to marry a common pirate. She sailed and fought with him, dressed in men's clothes. Later she fell in love with another pirate—who unfortunately turned out to be woman, Mary Read! When their ship was finally caught, they remained on deck to fight as the men ran to shelter below decks. When Anne's husband was being walked to the gallows she told him, 'I am grieved to see you in such straits. Had you fought like a man, you would not be hung like a dog!'

Madagascar was a notorious pirate lair in the 17th and 18th centuries and was the site of several pirate kingdoms. The outstanding one was the republic of Libertalia, an international libertarian society made up of people who shared a belief in the importance of freedom above all else. It was founded by the French pirate Misson and an Italian padre. The republic lived from capturing cargoes belonging to 'exploiting' merchants and grew crops and raised cattle. The official language was a sort of Esperanto (an international language). The Libertarians were eventually massacred by natives.

◀ Mary Read, shown here, came from a poor family and started her adventurous career as an army camp follower and a soldier's wife.

◀ The capture of Anne Bonny and Mary Read in 1720 did not deter women from engaging in piracy as shown by this engraving of Ann Mills who served in the frigate *Maidstone* in 1740.

▶ When threatened by attack from pirates many ships struck their colours and surrendered without a fight. If a fight started the crews fought with desperation because pirates seldom showed any mercy in an attack.

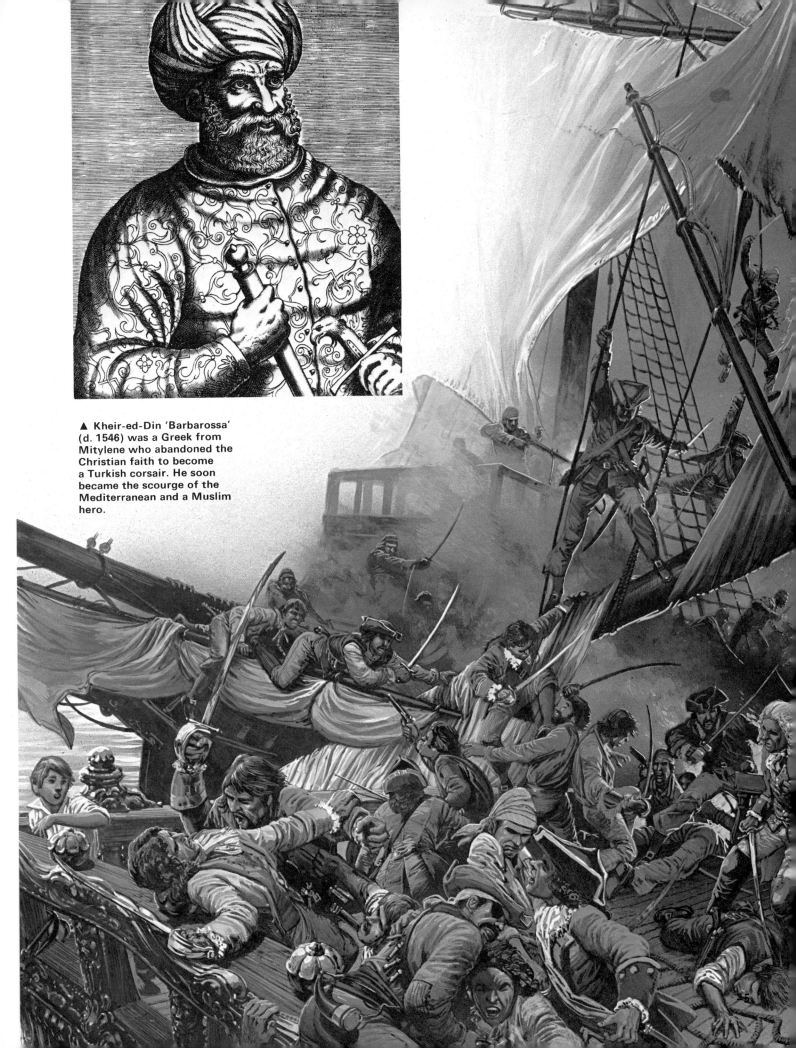

▲ Kheir-ed-Din 'Barbarossa' (d. 1546) was a Greek from Mitylene who abandoned the Christian faith to become a Turkish corsair. He soon became the scourge of the Mediterranean and a Muslim hero.

James Cook and the South Seas

In the second half of the 18th century between the Seven Years' War and the French Revolution, England and France sent out a number of maritime explorations under naval command. For the first time, the major purpose was the search for scientific knowledge instead of loot and plunder. These expeditions were led by men such as Wallis, Carteret, Cook and Vancouver for England and Bougainville, Marion-Dufresne, Kerguelen and La Perouse for France.

James Cook was not only the outstanding figure of the period but was probably the greatest navigator-explorer of all times. He was of humble birth and had been apprenticed to a shopkeeper before becoming a merchant seaman.

He sailed in Whitby colliers (small but stout coal-carrying ships engaged in the coastal trade). He later joined the Navy as an able seaman. He distinguished himself as a surveyor and a navigator during Wolfe's Quebec campaign. He had reached the rank of lieutenant when in 1768 he was offered the leadership of an expedition to the South Sea (Pacific). He had proposed using a Whitby collier, the *Endeavour*, because it was the most suitable type of ship.

The *Endeavour* sailed with 83 naval personnel and 11 civilians, mainly scientists who were directed by Sir Joseph Banks, a young naturalist of considerable wealth and ability. The destination was Cape Horn and Tahiti where astronomical surveys were to be carried out. The stay in Tahiti was idyllic and the men were sad to leave. Cook left for the second purpose

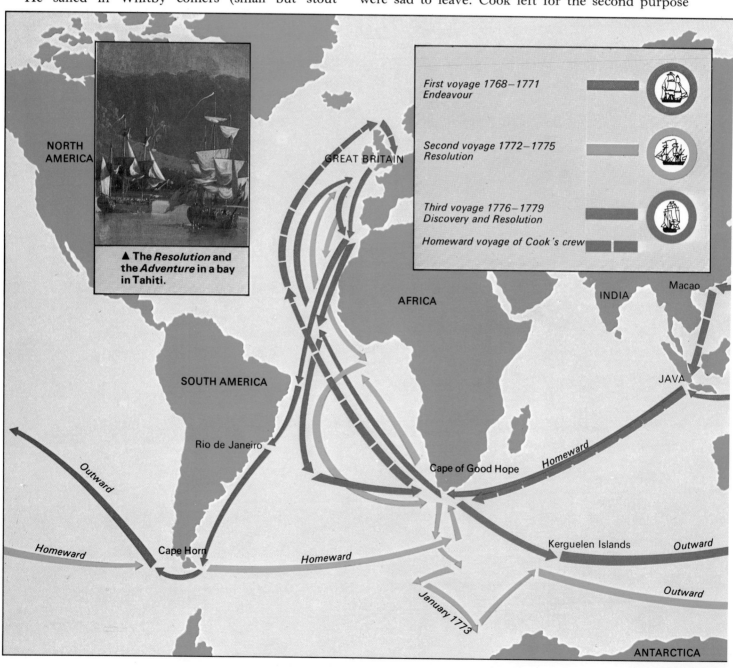

▲ The *Resolution* and the *Adventure* in a bay in Tahiti.

First voyage 1768–1771
Endeavour

Second voyage 1772–1775
Resolution

Third voyage 1776–1779
Discovery and Resolution

Homeward voyage of Cook's crew

NORTH AMERICA

GREAT BRITAIN

AFRICA

INDIA

Macao

SOUTH AMERICA

JAVA

Rio de Janeiro

Cape of Good Hope

Homeward

Outward

Homeward

Cape Horn

Homeward

Kerguelen Islands

Outward

January 1773

Outward

ANTARCTICA

of the expedition, which was to find the legendary southern continent of *Terra Australis Incognita*. Cook sailed to New Zealand which was thought to be the northern tip of the southern continent; he demonstrated that it was actually two large islands. He then discovered New South Wales and was almost shipwrecked on the Great Barrier Reef before sailing between Australia and New Guinea—which were previously thought to be one land.

He returned to England by way of Batavia and the Cape of Good Hope. A great welcome awaited him there and his reward was promotion to commander. In 1772 he set off again, with two other colliers, the *Resolution* and the *Adventure*. The aim this time was to search for *Terra Australis* further south. All Cook found was ice blocking his way. He therefore sailed north to New Zealand and Tahiti. A further attempt in the South Pacific reached the ice again, at 71° of latitude. Cook then criss-crossed the Pacific, passing or calling at Easter Island, Tahiti, the Marquesas, New Caledonia (which he discovered), Norfolk Island and New Zealand. He passed Cape Horn and discovered South Georgia and the South Sandwich Islands before sailing home to report that the famous *Terra Australis* did not exist.

In 1776 Cook sailed again, as post-captain, to seek the Northwest Passage from its Pacific side. He did not find it but charted the north-west coast of America and many islands. He also discovered Hawaii, where he was murdered by natives in 1779.

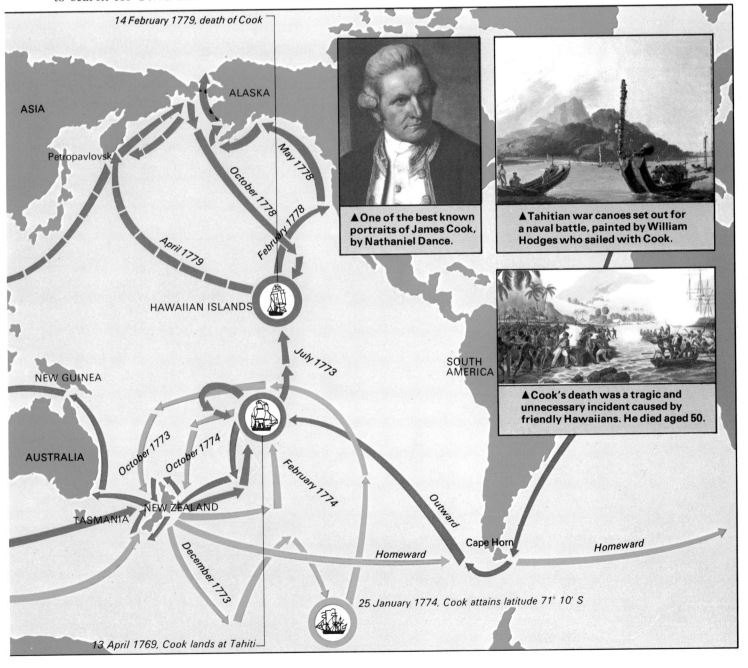

14 February 1779, death of Cook

ALASKA

ASIA

Petropavlovsk

May 1778

October 1778

February 1778

April 1779

HAWAIIAN ISLANDS

July 1773

NEW GUINEA

SOUTH AMERICA

October 1773

October 1774

February 1774

AUSTRALIA

TASMANIA   NEW ZEALAND

December 1773

Outward

Cape Horn

Homeward

Homeward

25 January 1774, Cook attains latitude 71° 10′ S

13 April 1769, Cook lands at Tahiti

▲One of the best known portraits of James Cook, by Nathaniel Dance.

▲Tahitian war canoes set out for a naval battle, painted by William Hodges who sailed with Cook.

▲Cook's death was a tragic and unnecessary incident caused by friendly Hawaiians. He died aged 50.

The East Indiamen

The East-Indiamen were the large merchant ships owned or operated by the rich and powerful East India companies. The two most important companies were the English Honourable East India Company and the Dutch East India Company. Their ships were much larger than other merchant vessels; they looked rather like ships-of-the-line, with two gun-decks, although the lower gun deck usually had no guns to make more space for cargoes. In fact the warships and cargo ships were so similar that many of the Dutch naval ships used during the Dutch wars were formerly East-Indiamen.

The East-Indiamen carried valuable cargoes and were built to resist the attacks of pirates and privateers who sailed the Indian Ocean. They were an attraction for marauders who occasionally attacked and sometimes succeeded in capturing them. On the other hand the appearance of the East-Indiamen sometimes kept enemy warships at bay. Their cargoes included wines and spirits, lead, copper, silver and manufactured wares outward-bound from Europe and tea, silks, spices and chinaware from India on the homeward voyage.

Officer appointments on these ships were much in demand because they held great social prestige and provided a very good income. Experience was not the only qualification for such posts; they also had to be bought.

An English captain could expect to pay £8,000 to secure his command but he could then look forward to an income of £2,000 a year. One captain even made £18,300 in just three voyages—a considerable fortune. Much of the revenue of Indiamen officers came from perks known as 'indulgencies'—the right to carry free of charge a specified weight of cargo for private speculation and resale. Thus Port and Madeira wines and specially brewed India Pale Ale (which were in great demand by the Europeans working for the Company in India) were carried on the way out and chinaware on the way back. Another source of income for the officers was the letting of their cabins at a very high price to some privileged passengers as there were no passenger cabins.

The best accommodation, on account of the prevailing winds, was in the port-side out and starboard home. It was from the initial letters of this expression that the word 'posh' originated. Even posh accommodation was by no means comfortable by today's standards. The cabins were small and the passengers were expected to provide not only their bedding but also their furniture. Cabin passengers dined at the captain's table and had the luxury of fresh meat and eggs provided by the livestock carried on deck. Other passengers were expected to bring their own food—for a passage that could last four to six months! They had to do their own cooking on their own portable spirit stoves which must have been a tremendous fire hazard. The alternative was to share the unappetizing food eaten by the seamen. Passengers were mainly Company employees such as administrators, buyers, soldiers and officers, but clergymen and missionaries were also often on the voyages to India.

◀ China tea chests are shown here being unloaded at London. Some chests also contained precious china packed in tea leaves.

Tea, drunk in China since 2737 BC, first reached England in AD 1657 and quickly became a major export from the East Indies.

▲ The *Vereenigde Oostindische Companie* was the Dutch East India Company (1602–1798) and its monogram VOC was reproduced on ships' ensigns, guns and trade articles.

◀ East Indiamen of the 'Blackwall frigate' type leaving St. Helena in 1830. The ship in the foreground is the *Inglis*.

Rum, sugar and slaves

The first transatlantic shipment of slaves took place in 1530, to Hispaniola, and the last one in 1888 to Brazil. During those 358 years an estimated 15 million negroes crossed the Atlantic in slave ships and perhaps as many as 9 million others did not survive the passage. At first only the Spaniards and the Portuguese were in the trade but the profits were very attractive and the English soon followed (in 1562), as well as the French, the Italians and the Dutch. In fact any country that could put a ship to sea traded in slaves, even if it did not have its own New World colony in need of slave labour.

Until the late 18th century the trade was not considered to be morally wrong; on the contrary it was a highly respectable business to be in, as well as a means of gaining wealth. However, more enlightened ideas grew steadily which resulted in the outlawing of the trade in 1807 for English ships. The other slave-trading countries copied this example in the following years. Although the trade was made illegal it was still carried on until 1888.

In the 17th and 18th centuries the slavers (as slave-ships were called) were engaged in a very profitable triangular trade—a voyage in three passages, all of which showed profits. The ships would fit out in such ports as Bristol in England, Nantes in France or Providence in Rhode Island and load 'trade goods' of brandy or rum, brightly printed cotton cloths, cheap muskets and glass beads. Then they would set sail to Africa, to a 'factory' where slaves were kept in barracoons (special sheds or enclosures for prisoners).

The slaves were mainly prisoners-of-war sold by the inland tribal chief to the factory agents, who were usually African themselves as Europeans seldom survived the climate and the fevers. Tribal warfare was of course often encouraged by the traders. They would pay handsomely, by local standards, for prisoners. After discussion, a rate of barter would be established between the agent and the slaver's master. For instance, two muskets, six powder kegs, two spirit kegs, one cat skin, two bags of lead, two plates and 12 knives would be exchanged for a healthy adult male slave; two boys or three girls could be obtained for the same goods.

When the terms had been agreed the slaves were taken on board ship and crammed into the hold, on tiered platforms where they were shackled to prevent any rush for freedom. After the trade was made illegal and the traders wanted to make as much profit from as few voyages as possible, the packing in of the slaves became truly horrible. The 25-metre long slaver *Vigilant* was arrested in 1822 with 476 slaves on board. Once well out to sea, the 'passengers' were unshackled and made to take exercise on deck and passable food was served to them: they had to be in a fit state to be sold at destination.

The passage lasted eight to ten weeks before the embargo and four to five weeks afterwards when faster vessels (to escape patrols) came into use. The death rate was high (as it was also on non-slaving voyages in the Tropics) for both slaves and crews, and was mainly due to contagious fevers which spread easily in the overcrowded ships. At destination the slaves were sold off at auction. They were usually paid for in goods—rum, sugar, molasses, tobacco or cotton (all produced by slaves)—which then became the return cargo.

▼ Slaves were packed side by side for the voyage on tiered shelves or platforms built inside the hold. Any form of movement was difficult. They were shackled to prevent them from escaping by diving overboard. Many slaves died during the voyage.

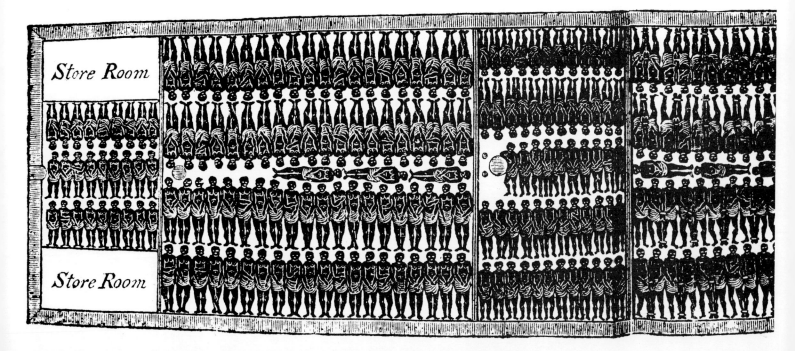

Store Room

Store Room

▲ In an attempt to keep the 'cargo' healthy, the slaves were made to exercise daily on deck and forced to dance.

▼ The inside of a slave trader as painted by a naval lieutenant who captured her in 1830.

▲ A waxwork model of William Wilberforce who lived from 1759 to 1833 and was the son of a wealthy Hull merchant. In 1788 with the help of Clarkson and the Quakers, he led the movement which was to succeed in outlawing the slave trade in 1807.

▼ Map of the triangular trade which started from Europe. The slavers would carry goods to be exchanged in Africa for slaves. The slaves were sold in the West Indies and the southern part of North America. On the final stage of the journey rum and sugar would be transported to Europe.

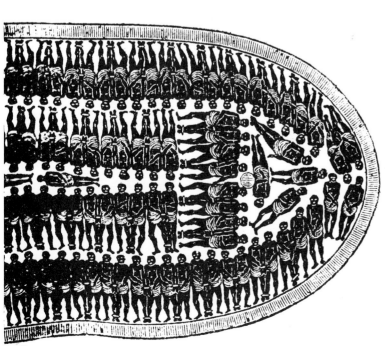

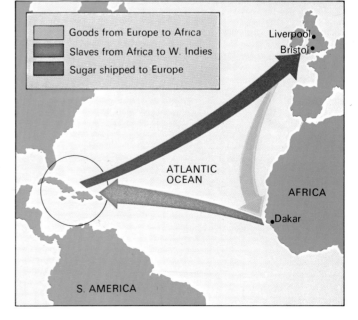

Goods from Europe to Africa

Slaves from Africa to W. Indies

Sugar shipped to Europe

Liverpool

Bristol

ATLANTIC OCEAN

AFRICA

Dakar

S. AMERICA

Men-o'-war

The men-o'-war, as warships were called in the days of sail, were classed by the number of their guns. From the 1650s the ships with two or three gun-decks were called ships-of-the-line or liners because they would form a line or column when attacking an enemy fleet, so that they could protect one another. The largest liners were called first-rates and had more than a 100 guns. There were never many of these because they were extremely expensive to build and to man.

Nelson's *Victory* is such a first-rate and the only liner preserved to this day. She took 2,500 oak trees to build and had a crew of 842 men; she is 70 metres long and has 104 guns. Her poop, the uppermost deck, extends from the stern to just forward of the mizzen mast. This deck was only lightly armed with two 12 pounder guns (firing shots weighing 12 lbs, 5.4 kilos) and two 68 pounder carronades, stubby guns firing heavy shots (31 kilos) but with a short range.

Below the poop are the captain's quarters and forward of these, on the level, is the quarter-deck, with the double steering wheel. It was armed with twelve 12 pounder guns (including those in the captain's quarters). The quarter-deck extends forward to the main-mast and is linked to the fo'c'sle, (forecastle—a raised deck at the same level and at the fore end of the ship) by two catwalks, the gangways, to port and starboard. The space between the quarter-deck, the gangways and the fo'c'sle is like a well opening on the upper gun-deck below where the ship's boats are carried.

HMS Victory, launched on May 7 1765

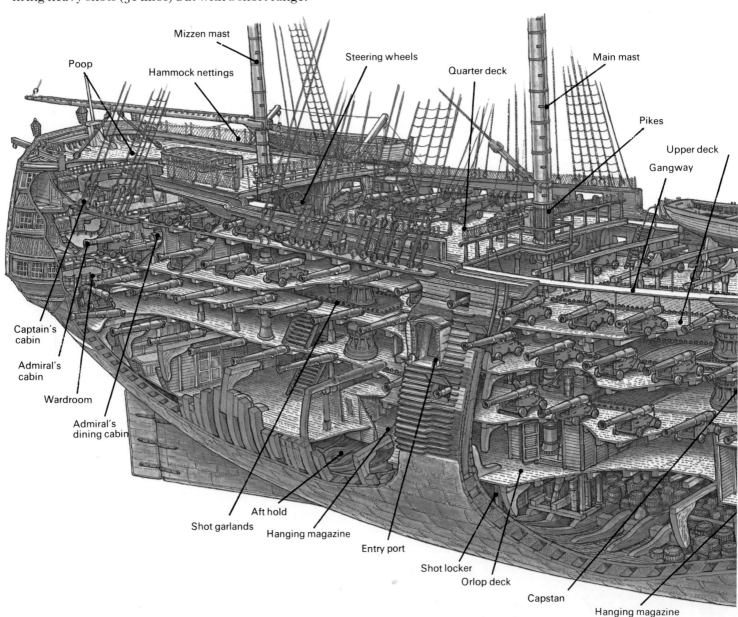

The fo'c'sle carries two 12 pounder guns and two 68 pounder carronades. Below this level is the upper gun-deck with thirty 12 pounder guns and its after part is partitioned off for the admiral's quarters. The middle gun-deck, below, carries twenty-eight 24 pounder (10.8 kilo) guns and its after part is called the officers' wardroom. The lower gun-deck, below, has the heaviest armament, thirty 32 pounder (14.4 kilo) guns, and its after part is called the gun-room and is the junior midshipmen's quarters.

The seamen slept in hammocks in the middle and lower gun-decks. The deck under the lower gun-deck, the orlop, is below waterline. It contains the powder magazines, the bread-room, the cable tiers (where the anchor cable was coiled up) and the after-cockpit which was the senior midshipmen's berth. It was also where the wounded were treated by the surgeon during battle. Below the orlop is the hold which was filled with water casks, salt beef and pork casks, salt fish, spare cordage and shot.

First-and second-rate ships had three gun-decks like the *Victory*; third-and fourth-rates only had two gun-decks. Warships with only one gun-deck were not powerful enough to be part of the line-of-battle. These were frigates, with 22 to 44 (or more) guns, and smaller sloops-of-war (both of which were ship-rigged, with three masts, all with square sails), or brigs (with two masts, both with square sails), or schooners (with two masts, fore-and-aft rig). These vessels were used as fleet auxiliaries, for patrols or for carrying despatches.

▶ HMS *Victory* at her dock in Portsmouth Dockyard, where she has been restored to her 1805 appearance.

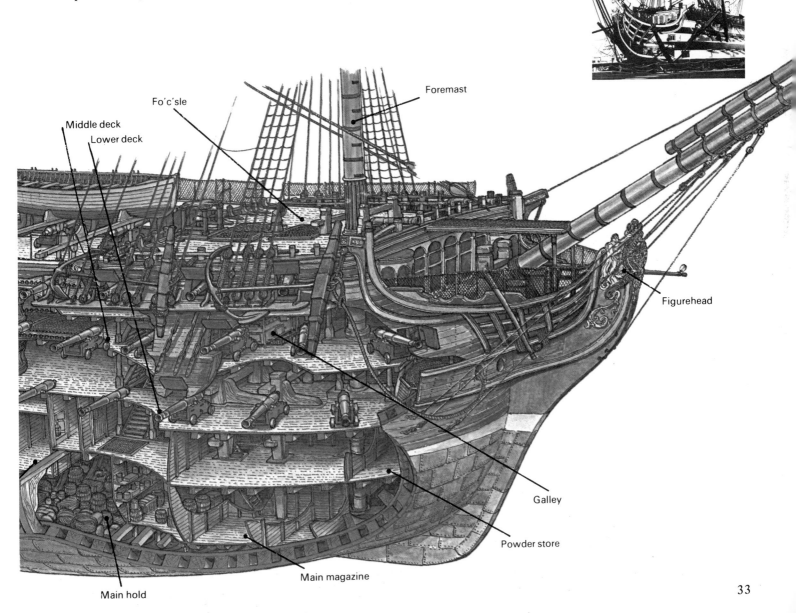

Foremast

Fo'c'sle

Middle deck

Lower deck

Figurehead

Galley

Powder store

Main magazine

Main hold

33

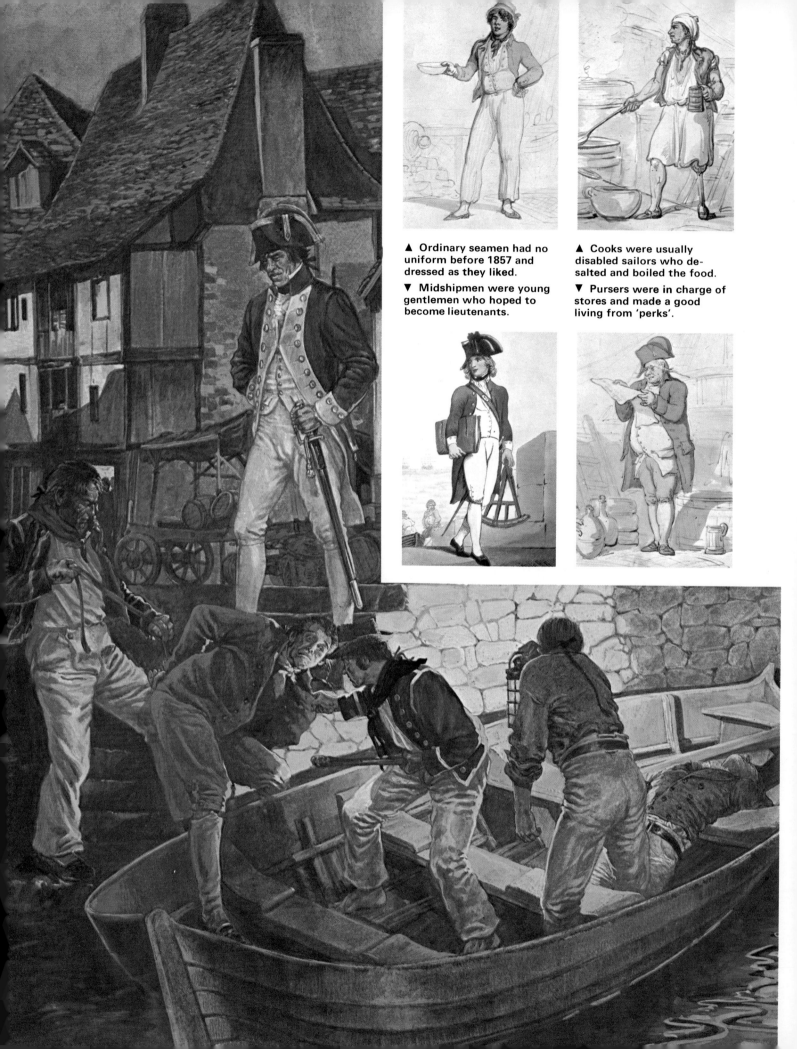

▲ Ordinary seamen had no uniform before 1857 and dressed as they liked.

▼ Midshipmen were young gentlemen who hoped to become lieutenants.

▲ Cooks were usually disabled sailors who de-salted and boiled the food.

▼ Pursers were in charge of stores and made a good living from 'perks'.

Nelson's navy

The French Revolutionary and Napoleonic Wars were the classic age of fighting sail. During this period large fleet actions such as the Battle of the Nile, of Copenhagen and of Trafalgar took place, as well as countless frigate duels and privateering engagements.

Few professional seamen volunteered for the Navy where the discipline was harder and the wages lower than in the merchant service. Thus the Navy would resort to impressment (the 'press') to man its fleets. Homeward-bound merchantmen were stopped by naval warships at sea and some of their prime seamen might be transferred by force to a naval ship. Convicted criminals were sent from the prisons to the King's ships. These men were rough and tough 'landlubbers' of the worst kind but with time and naval discipline they could be made into good fighting seamen. When there was a great shortage of hands the Navy resorted to the sending out of press-gangs to raid the waterfront inns and the quays to kidnap all the able-bodied men they could catch.

The sailors were kept in the service for as long as they were needed—and with the Napoleonic Wars lasting 22 years, many spent most of their active lives on men-o'-war. To prevent desertion, shore leave was seldom granted and some 'Jack Tars' (the sailors' nickname) spent four years or more without setting foot on dry land. Sea duty consisted mainly of patrols and blockade stations. Life on board was governed by a strict routine. The crews were divided into two watches which alternated for duty four hours on, four hours off; even when off watch, there were general duties during daytime.

The food was monotonous and bad. Breakfast consisted of *burgoo*, a sort of gluey, inferior porridge, and coffee made from roasted barley. Dinner and supper, served at noon and at 4pm, were identical. It was salt pork on Sundays and Thursdays, salt beef on Tuesdays and Saturdays, and meat was replaced by butter and cheese on the three remaining days. Dried peas or beans, oatmeal, small beer (weak beer) and rock-hard biscuits (usually infested with weevils) were the daily additions to the salt meat, which was usually very old and unpleasant. Grog—watered rum—was served in generous rations after dinner and supper, with a daily issue of lime-juice to protect sailors against scurvy.

Discipline was harsh and corporal punishments were commonplace. Casual whippings with rope-ends or rattans (canes) were given on the spot for minor misbehaviour and more serious offences were punished by flogging with a cat-o'-nine-tails.

When an enemy sail was sighted, a marine drummer would beat the drums. The sail-handling crews took their stations; the gun crews loaded and ran out the guns; the topmen manned the tops, armed with muskets or swivel-guns, and the marines lined the rails with their muskets. Boarding pikes and cutlasses were issued to the boarding parties—and the surgeon prepared his amputation saws in the orlop deck . . .

◄ **Until the end of the Napoleonic wars the Royal Navy resorted to press gangs to man the fleet whenever there was a shortage of volunteers.**

▼ **Nelson was fatally wounded at the start of the Battle of Trafalgar by a musket ball fired from the *Redoubtable*. He died knowing England had won.**

Privateers

A privateer was a privately owned ship (or any member of her crew) that had a special document, called a 'letter of marque and reprisal', which was issued by the State. It entitled the ship to attack enemy shipping (or harbours) during a time of war, but only under the conditions of time and place specified in the document.

Seized vessels could not be plundered as pirates did, but had (unless totally impracticable) to be brought back to the privateer's base. Here a court judged whether it was a 'fair prize' or should not have been seized. In the latter case the ship had to be returned to her owners. In the case of the 'fair prize', the ship and her cargo were put up for auction and the proceeds were split between the privateer's shareholders and the crew. The State first took away a large amount under the guise of various administrative fees. The seamen received no wages and depended on prize-money to make a living. The pickings were rarely large.

The most brilliant Dutch privateer was Piet Heyn. In 1628, while sailing as a commodore of a privateering fleet commissioned by the Dutch West India Company, he captured the entire Spanish silver fleet off Matanzas in Cuba. The booty was double the previous capital of the Company!

Jean Bart was a French privateer of Dunkirk in the days of Louis XIV. He went to sea at the age of 12 and had his own command at the age of 23; by the time he was 27 he was a very wealthy man. When captured by the English, he managed to escape from Portsmouth and rowed back to France in a small boat.

Another French privateer of the same period was René Duguay-Trouin from St Malo. René was only 16 years old when he allowed his captain to capture a ship even though the captain considered abandoning the chase because it appeared too heavily armed: René had noticed that most of the enemy guns were dummies! In the ensuing fight Duguay-Trouin also distinguished himself by his valour. He too was made a prisoner and escaped by rowing boat from Plymouth. Later he became a post-captain in the regular French Navy and in 1711 held to ransom the town of Rio de Janeiro.

Woodes Rogers was an English privateer who made a memorable circumnavigation in 1708–11. He raided the Spanish towns of the Pacific coast of America, capturing many prizes. Thomas Boyle is one of the best known of the many American privateers of the War of 1812. He snatched a ship and a brig and disabled another brig while keeping at bay a man-o'-war.

Robert Surcouf, a St Malo privateer, was a hero of the Napoleonic Wars. The scene of his most brilliant exploits was the Indian Ocean and his most famous prize, in 1800, was the East-Indiaman *Kent* which was three times the size of his own *Confiance* and which carried a cargo valued at £75,000.

▲ In 1807 William Rogers, master of the mail packet *Windsor Castle*, leading the boarders against an attacking French privateer.

▼ Jean Bart of Dunkirk, a famous French privateer. He attacked Dutch fishing fleets and raided the north east coast of England.

▶ Woodes Rogers and his men stripping the jewellery off the Spanish ladies of Guayaguil (in today's Ecuador). They did not molest their victims, unlike pirates who were often cruel to their prisoners.

▼ Captain Morgan's ships here engaged in battle with Spanish frigates attempting to prevent his escape after attacking Maracaibo in Venezuela. Between the 16th and 18th centuries the West Indies and harbours along the northern coast of South America were pirate and privateer strongholds and consequently attacks on them were frequent.

'Thar she blows!'

In the days of sail five species of whale were hunted, mainly the right whale, in Arctic waters, and the sperm whale, in tropical waters. By the early 19th century the stocks of whales in the Atlantic were running low and whaling ships—mainly from New England—were fitted out for campaigns lasting several years. These ships went on voyages to the Pacific and Indian Oceans. They would only return when they had a full cargo of whale oil, used for soap-making and for oil lamps. They had crews of 30 to 50 men who signed on not for a wage but for a share of the profits.

Lookouts were stationed aloft and when a tell-tale spout was sighted they would cry 'Thar she blows!' and give the distance and bearing. The whale-boats, ready on the davits (cranes for lowering boats) were lowered into the water; each boat was manned by a crew of six. They carried three harpoons, three lances, and water and provisions, in case they lost the mother ship. They had a removable mast, sail and rudder which were fixed and replaced by five pulling oars and a steering oar for the attack. The whale was harpooned and to the harpoon was fixed a 220-fathom line coiled in a bucket; another bucket contained a spare 100-fathom line which could be added if the whale sounded (dived) too deeply. Sometimes the harpooned whale would tow the boat in a wild frenzied bid for escape but it seldom turned around to attack its tormentors. Eventually when it lay exhausted on the surface it was killed with a lance.

The whale was lashed alongside the ship and flensed (peeled) from a stage rigged above it, by men wielding sharp blades on long poles. The blubber was flensed spiral fashion, making a blanket-piece which was hoisted on board by large tackles fixed to the main mast. It was cut up in chunks ('Bibles') and then in slivers ('Bible leaves') which were thrown into the trypots (big cauldrons encased in a brick furnace on deck) to be melted into oil. The fire was fed by scraps of melted blubber. A full shipload of about 2,500 barrels of oil represented the killing of some 30 whales.

The Arctic whalers operated in much the same way but sailed for the summer only and brought back the blubber for processing ashore. In 1870 the Norwegian Sven Foyn invented the harpoon gun, which was mounted in the bows of powered ships. It allowed the wholesale slaughter of a further seven species of whales. Modern whaling, mainly Russian and Japanese, uses factory ships supplied by fleets of catcher ships, and the whales are mercilessly tracked down by sonar and helicopters.

Current studies of whales and their smaller relatives, the dolphins, show that these animals are extraordinarily intelligent. Many species of whales killed for commercial use are on the verge of extinction and the protection of these creatures is an important aim of conservation today.

▲ The sea around Greenland was the centre of much whale fishing and is often mentioned in whaling folk songs. Here fishermen earlier this century drag in a whale prior to processing.

◀ The 'boat steerer' (who is not the 'steersman' at the oar) is about to give a sperm whale another 'iron' because the first harpoon and line have broken. Hand harpoons do not kill the whales but are like fish hooks on lines when game fishing. When the whales are exhausted and can be approached they are killed by lance thrusts.

The advent of steam

All too often wind is a commodity of which there is either not enough or too much, or which blows from the wrong direction. Since ancient times man's attempt to free himself from reliance upon the wind has produced amongst other inventions, the paddle, the oar, and even the paddle-wheel. But until the 19th century the power supplying the movement was restricted to human and animal muscle. And these low-powered and inefficient engines consumed enormous quantities of expensive fuel known as food!

The energy contained in steam had been recognized for a number of centuries but practical ways of harnessing it were not discovered until the early 18th century. The first attempt to use steam on a boat was made by an Englishman, Jonathan Hulls, in 1737; it failed because of insufficient power. It was only in 1783 that the Frenchman Jouffroy d'Abbans produced the first working steamboat, the *Pyroscaphe*, which sailed on the river Saône, but at considerable financial loss.

The next landmark in the history of steam was the *Charlotte Dundas*. She was built in 1801 by the Scotsman William Symmington as a barge tug for the Forth and Clyde Canal. She had a stern paddle-wheel powered by a 10 horsepower direct-acting cylinder. Her potential was not realized because the canal owners restricted her use, for they were worried that the paddle wash would wear away the canal banks.

In 1807, Fulton, an American engineer, built the first economically successful steamboat, the *Clermont*, for the Hudson River service. The first coastal passage under steam was made in 1808 by the PS (Paddle-steamer) *Phoenix*, from New York to Philadelphia. The first European commercial service, on the Clyde, was opened by Bell's *Comet* in 1812. The PS *Savannah* was built in 1818 as a pure sailing ship and was sold, before her launching to new owners who fitted her with a steam engine of an old design. When they realized that they could neither use her nor sell her in the United States, they sailed her across the Atlantic, using the engine for only 13 per cent of the passage time, to try to sell her in Europe.

The first Atlantic crossing under steam was made in 1838 by the PS *Sirius* at a 6.7 knots average. (A knot is a nautical mile per hour. 10 knots equal about 18.5km/h). Within hours of her triumphant arrival at New York, Isambard Brunel's PS *Great Western* steamed in, having crossed the ocean at 8.8 knots average. The *Great Western* was the first successful ocean steam liner, sailing until 1857. The next step forward was made by another Brunel ship, the *Great Britain* in 1843, which was the first screw-propelled, iron-built ship to cross the Atlantic. She is now being restored and preserved at the dock where she was launched, in Bristol. The *Great Eastern*, the last of Brunel's innovations was launched in 1858.

▲ A cutaway drawing of Brunel's *Great Britain* shows one of the boilers and the steam pipes to the engine in which four fixed cylinders turn the crankshaft. The propeller is turned by the shaft driven from the small wheel by chains from the bigger wheel on the crankshaft. The ship was the first to be built entirely of iron although the hull was covered with wooden planking outside the metal. The six masts carried sails which were designed to steady the ship at sea to reduce the roll of the hull rather than to drive her.

► An artist's impression of the paddle engines of Brunel's *Great Eastern*.

▲ Isambard Kingdom Brunel was a civil engineer rather than a naval architect. He constructed tunnels, bridges, railways and ships. He designed the *Great Western* (1838), the second steamship to cross the Atlantic; the *Great Britain* (1843), a screw-propellered steamer, and the *Great Eastern* (1858), the largest vessel ever built in those times.

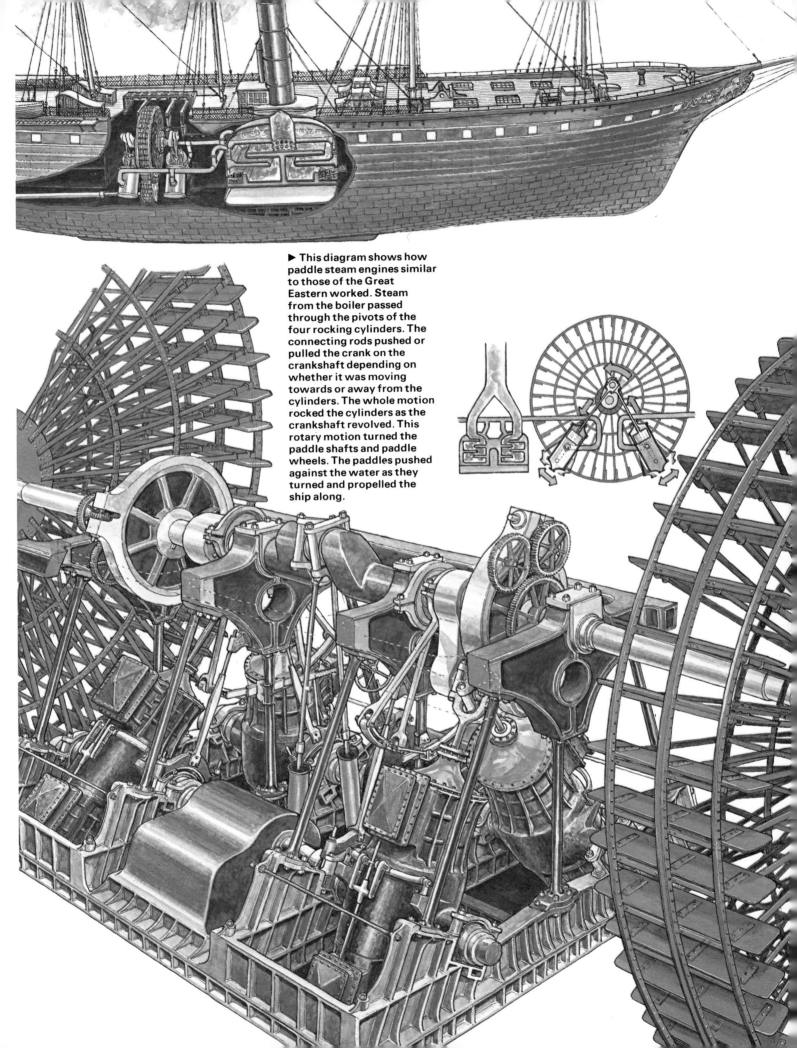

▶ This diagram shows how paddle steam engines similar to those of the Great Eastern worked. Steam from the boiler passed through the pivots of the four rocking cylinders. The connecting rods pushed or pulled the crank on the crankshaft depending on whether it was moving towards or away from the cylinders. The whole motion rocked the cylinders as the crankshaft revolved. This rotary motion turned the paddle shafts and paddle wheels. The paddles pushed against the water as they turned and propelled the ship along.

Emigrant ships

Emigrant sailing ships in the 19th century were seldom specially designed for the purpose. Even those that *were* built for the trade differed little from other merchant ships of the time, except that their poop deck sheltering the cabin accommodation was longer than in other ships. The 'first class' area consisted of cabins built around the saloon where the cabin passengers dined with the ship's officers. The cabins were cramped and only rarely contained such luxury as a washstand.

The passengers were expected to provide their own bedding—including the mattress—and any furniture they might be able to fit in. There were usually no toilet facilities apart from chamber-pots. Passages were long—about a month to America and four months to Australia. At least the cabin passengers were served daily with fresh produce from a large number of animals carried on deck. A ship bound for Australia in 1863 with 42 cabin passengers and 240 'tween-deck passengers carried 28 sheep, 18 pigs, a sow in litter, 240 hens, 120 ducks, 48 geese, 96 turkeys, a cow and a calf for ship-board use, plus 36 rams, 3 dogs, 20 rabbits and 2 horses for export. Few of the wealthy cabin passengers were emigrants. Most were travelling on business, for leisure or study, but even so, their conditions of travel were far from comfortable.

The 'tween-deck' (the upper level of the ship's hold) was used for carrying cargo on return passages and was converted to immigrant use by building disposable tiered bunks with rough boards. This packed dormitory was divided into three compartments. Single men slept forward, married couples and their children amidships and single women aft. The crowding and insanitary conditions were almost as bad as on slave-ships and contagious diseases spread rapidly. Fresh water was strictly rationed and one can imagine the awful smell of the quarters situated just below the farmyard on deck.

When weather was bad—and that could last for days on end—the emigrants were shut in down below deck, without light, air or the means of cooking food. These passengers had to bring their own food for the passage and those who had spent their last pennies on the fare would almost starve to death (and sometimes actually did) at sea, particularly if the ship was delayed. The livestock was not available to them and the master was loath to sell some of the ship's crew's provisions. The 'tween-deck people also had to do their own cooking, in their own pannikins, on a fire-rack on deck. These emigrants had chosen to emigrate—to avoid the poverty and starvation at home—but few could have imagined how bad their voyages would be.

▲ British emigrants bound for America. The conditions on emigrant ships were extremely crowded. The food was poor but the passengers' hopes for a bright new future were high.

▼ The 'tween deck of an emigrant ship bound for Sydney in 1844. The tables, benches and bunks were dismantled to allow space for wool cargo on the return run.

◄ 'The last of England' by Ford Madox Brown. This medallion depicts the fears of emigrants who are leaving their homeland, probably for ever.

► A Black Ball liner, a clipper typical of the sailing ships used on the North Atlantic emigrant passage. They were the fastest ships of the day and started out mostly from Liverpool which was the principal port from which emigrants embarked.

Glory of sail: the clippers

'To clip along' means to sail fast and the word clipper was loosely applied to all fast sailing ships before the clipper era. It was particularly used for the late 18th century to early 19th century 'Baltimore clippers,' which were usually rigged as topsail schooners. These ships were employed as privateers, slavers or smugglers, all of which required a good turn of speed.

As early as 1815 some of these American ships were challenging the English East India Company's monopoly of the China trade which was smuggling opium in and exporting tea. These American 'China packets' soon grew in size and rig, becoming brigs and fully-rigged ships in the period 1830–45, but retaining the fast hull shapes of the earlier schooners. The China trade itself expanded in 1842 with the opening of more Chinese harbours.

In 1845 the American naval architect J. W. Griffiths produced the China packet *Rainbow*, which had a number of design innovations to improve speed. At the same time Nat Palmer was building a similar ship, the *Houqua*. The trend was pushed to its conclusion by Griffiths in 1846 with his ship *Sea Witch*. Her clean flaring bows and convex stern lines made her typical of a new style of ship, where space had been decreased to increase speed. These were the unbelievably beautiful clippers with graceful hulls and towering pyramids of canvas, that we think of when we use the term 'clipper' today.

1849 was the year of the California Gold Rush and of the repeal of the English Navigation Acts. American ships were now allowed to carry tea to England. Commerce was in full boom, the emphasis was on speed and there was great shipbuilding activity. The following few years were those of the extreme-clippers which could pay for their high building costs and make a profit on their first voyage to San Francisco. With the added help of the newly published pilot charts, showing currents and prevailing winds, the new clippers smashed all previous passage records. The clippers could sail from New York to San Francisco round Cape Horn in less than 100 days where other ships took about 150 days. They were sailed by tough masters who drove large, unruly but competent crews.

By 1855 the heyday of the Gold Rush and of the extreme-clippers had passed but medium-clippers were being built in America for English shipowners. In 1857 America was in the grip of a trade depression and her shipbuilding never properly recovered before the Civil War.

This war ended America's brilliant lead in building and sailing ships. By then England was building her own clippers, using composite construction (planks fastened to iron frames) to overcome the shortage of timber. These last composite clippers were still beautiful ships and continued to break passage records.

It was to beat the superb *Thermopylae* that the *Cutty Sark* was built at Dumbarton in 1869. The British clippers couldn't achieve the speeds of the American-built clippers which could reach 20 or 21 knots and cover approximately 650 km in the course of 24 hours. The British clippers could, however, sail at the speed of 17 knots and cover 580 km in 24 hours.

► The wheel, compass, binnacle and rigging of the clipper ship *Cutty Sark*, which is now preserved at Greenwich in London. It was built in 1869 and began by carrying tea from China.

▼ Large men-o'-war and prestige ships had bows decorated by a figurehead, the origin of which goes back to prehistoric magic beliefs. The figurehead shown here is that of the China tea clipper *Lalla Rooke*.

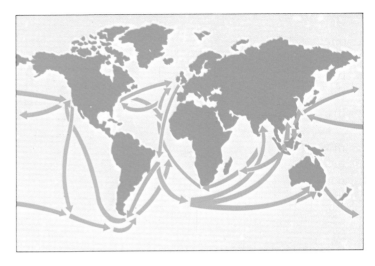

▲ A map of the main clipper ship routes. These were from the American East Coast and Western Europe to San Francisco via Cape Horn, to China or Australia via the Cape of Good Hope.

The routes used by clippers were dictated by 'trade' winds, which changed according to the season.

Main Clipper Routes

▼ The British clipper ship *Anglesey*, 1150 tons. The ship is on the port tack with all sails set except the topgallant sails. The clippers first made their name by carrying passengers to California during the great gold rush.

Danger round Cape Horn

After entering the Pacific through the Strait of Magellan in 1578 Francis Drake was blown southeastward by a storm, thus accidentally discovering the open passage between the Atlantic and the Pacific. In 1616 the Dutchman Schouten was the next to use this passage on his way to the East Indies. He named the southernmost island and promontory Hoorn, after his home town.

Cape Horn is situated at about 55°S at the southernmost tip of South America, where it is almost continually exposed to westerly gales and storms. These winds circle the globe without being stopped by land masses and are funnelled in Drake's Passage, between Cape Horn and Antarctica. In the summer icebergs and fog contribute to the danger to shipping while in winter the days are short and the whipping rain often turns into snow-storms. The ships become covered in ice and the ropes freeze in their blocks. But this grim Passage was preferable to the Strait of Magellan with its steep lee shores, strong tidal currents and fogs.

Until the California Gold Rush the Cape Horn route was not often used but it then became one of the great seaways, eventually becoming the last stronghold of deep-water sailing. Rounding the Horn was calculated to be from 50°S in the Atlantic to 50°S in the Pacific. Sometimes the headwinds are so bad that ships could spend a month or more in the freezing storm-lashed Drake's Passage. Many ships were dismasted or lost and some turned tail to sail east-about. 'Doubling the Horn' from west to east took a much shorter time but was no less dangerous. The huge following and breaking seas constantly threatened to crash over a ship's stern, which often meant that the wheel, the boats, the galley and all the men on deck were swept away. And there was always the danger that the ship might be flung sideways to the seas and capsized.

From the 1860s the clippers began to be replaced by big iron, and then steel, ships and barques with up to five masts. These huge windjammers were more strongly built than the wooden ships but they were heavier and rode the waves less easily and often sustained heavy damage in the Cape Horn storms. They had a rounder shape of underwater hull than the clippers but were just as fast, owing to their greater length. Working on board the windjammers was harder as they carried fewer crew members than the clippers did.

The windjammers were used primarily in the Chilean nitrate and Peruvian guano (fertilizer) trades until 1914; these trips included a Cape Horn passage both ways. Windjammers were also used to carry Australian grain until 1949, circling the globe at each voyage. All the other deep sea trades were by now carried out by steam ships. Germany and Finland were the last two countries to send square-riggers round Cape Horn.

The last two roundings of the Horn by windjammers carrying a commercial cargo were undertaken by the 4-masted barques *Pamir* and *Passat*, under the Finnish flag. The world will never see such ships and seamen again; the modern sail-training tall ships cannot really compare with them for excitement and atmosphere.

◄ Stormy weather on a large steel windjammer. Life lines and life nets have been rigged to prevent seamen from being swept overboard.

▼ The four-masted barque *Pamir* was built in 1905 for the Chilean saltpetre trade and was the last cargo-carrying sailing ship to go around Cape Horn in 1949. As a schoolship, she was tragically lost in 1957.

◄ The barque *Pamir* at anchor in a gale. All the sails are furled except the lower spanker to keep the ship head into the wind.

► Furling sails on a square-rigger requires a good team who work together to lift up and roll the heavy canvas into a tight bundle on top of the yard. Each man needs a good **sense** of balance and a head for heights.

The *Pamir* built in Hamburg, Germany in 1905

▲ The men are seen here hauling on **the clewlines** and buntlines to spill the wind out of a sail and to gather the sail up against its yard prior to furling.

Disasters at sea

The unsinkable ship does not exist. The sea, in her nastier moods, can wreck anything afloat. Even the best found powered ship can be blown onto shore, broken up at sea or capsize and flounder. In high latitudes icebergs take their toll and freezing spray or rain can add so much weight to the upperworks of ships that they can capsize. Many whaling or exploring vessels are hemmed in and crunched by pack ice.

Many disasters are not due to the elements but to navigational errors, fires, explosions, collisions, acts of war and other human or mechanical failures. Thousands of lives are lost at sea each year despite safety regulations and other improvements. In 1957 the German 4-masted training barque *Pamir*, after loading up with barley at Buenos Aires was caught in hurricane Carrie. Her cargo shifted, making her capsize and founder, with the loss of 91 men and boys out of her full crew of 97.

In 1816 the French frigate *Méduse* ran aground in fair weather on the Argun Bank off Mauretania, West Africa. Her captain and the officers took to the six boats with picked crews, leaving 150 women, soldiers, passengers and crew to fend for themselves on a makeshift raft which sank to waist level under their weight. They had hardly any water or food. During the next 13 days there were mutinies, murders, acts of folly and cannibalism. Only 15 survivors remained on the awful raft when it was found by a brig.

In 1967 the supertanker *Torrey Canyon* was stranded on the Seven Stones reef off Land's End and her tanks were ripped open. Over 20,000 tons of crude oil escaped and formed an oil slick covering over 670 sq. km. This accident was only one of the first of many similar oil-polluting disasters, which put wildlife and coasts in great danger.

The most famous of all sea disasters happened in 1912. The *Titanic*, thought to be unsinkable, sank on her maiden voyage after a collision with an iceberg. She carried only enough lifeboats for half the number of people on board (which was legal) and many of these boats could not be launched because of the listing of the sinking ship. To make matters worse, through lack of order and discipline, some lifeboats were launched with less than their full capacity of passengers. There were only 705 survivors out of 2207 people. This terrible disaster led to the re-writing of safety rules and to the creation of the International Ice Patrol.

Another famous liner disaster was the torpedoing of the *Lusitania* in 1915, by the German submarine U-20, with the loss of 1201 people out of 2160. More recently poor standards of crew and equipment were responsible for the loss of 128 lives following a fire on the Greek liner *Lakonia* on a Christmas cruise to the Canary Islands in 1963. The *Lakonia* sank after the survivors had been taken off.

▶ Fire on board a ship is a terrible disaster but fire on board an oil tanker is much worse because of the nature of the cargo. This tanker fire occurred at Bantry Bay in January 1979.

▼ Passengers leap into the river after a collision between the *Bywell Castle* and the *Princess Alice*, a pleasure steamer. The accident occurred in September 1878 on the River Thames and over 558 passengers were lost.

▶ Some of the 705 survivors from the *Titanic* disaster who were picked up by the liner *Carpathia*. The icy waters of the Atlantic claimed 1,513 lives.

▼ The crew have a makeshift picnic as they wait for the tide to float off their shipwrecked trawler *Reginald* which ran aground on St. Mary's in the Scillies in 1902.

▲ The S.S. *Titanic* on her trials in 1912. She was the largest and most luxurious liner to have been built at the time and was thought to be unsinkable.

▲ Commander Edward J. Smith captain of the *Titanic* on her maiden voyage.

Floating palaces

The success, in 1838, of the *Great Western* (see page 40) led the admiralty to ask for tenders for the carrying of mails between England and North America. The tender which was accepted, was submitted by Samuel Cunard, from Nova-Scotia. This was the beginning of the world's most famous liner company. Cunard's first ship in the service was the *Britannia*, a paddle-steamer with a barque rig, of 1135 tons, with a cruising speed of 8.5 knots and accommodation for 115 cabin passengers.

The trend was set away from the cramped conditions of the sailing packet ships. Everything was designed with the aim of making the passengers forget they were at sea. On the transoceanic runs the paddlers disappeared in 1860. As engines became increasingly reliable the liners finally shed their sailing rigs in the 1890s and acquired their modern look; at this time too multiple propellers came into use.

In 1907 the 31,550-ton *Lusitania* and *Mauretania* were launched for Cunard. They were the first such ships to be fitted with the faster and quieter steam turbines. In 1909 the *Mauretania* gained the 'Blue Riband', the distinction for the fastest Atlantic crossing, with a speed of 26.06 knots. She kept this award for the next 20 years. Her first-class cuisine was as good as that of the famous restaurants in the world's capitals. The lounge, tea room, smoking room and bars were as luxurious as those of the palatial hotels ashore, and the spacious cabins were furnished with refinement and comfort.

The liners carried orchestras and there were dances, galas and many other entertainments. Other famous luxury liners of the pre-1914 period were the *Olympic* and *Titanic* (1911–12, 46,000 tons), the *Imperator* (1912, 52,000 tons), the *Aquitania* (1914, 46,000 tons) and the *Vaterland* (1914, 46,000 tons). Many of these liners were used during World War I as armed merchant cruisers or as troop-ships, and several, including some in civilian use, were sunk.

The surviving liners were put back into service after 1918 (the German *Imperator* and *Bismark* having been seized by Britain and renamed *Berengeria* and *Majestic*). New liners were built to replace the lost or ageing ships to cope with the increasing numbers of passengers. The prestigious French *Normandie* (83,423 tons) was put into service in 1933. This was one year before Cunard's *Queen Mary* (82,070 tons) which was the passengers' all-time favourite. Her sistership, the *Queen Elizabeth*, was only completed in 1940 and started her career as a troop-ship. The American liner *United States*, (53,000 tons) was put in service in 1952.

Although the number of surface passengers reached a peak in 1957, air transport was by then becoming popular and with in the next ten years demand for passages on board the liners decreased.

The *France* (66,000 tons) launched in 1960 was one of the last traditional transatlantic liners. The *QE2* (65,900 tons) built in 1968, is now the only remaining passenger ship on the North Atlantic, and she sails to New York in summer months only. She is primarily a holiday-cruise ship and life on board, despite the luxurious interior, is not quite as stylish as on the liners of the first half of the 20th century.

1. The *Queen Elizabeth* 2 at Cowes in the Isle of Wight. This liner was built in 1969. It is 293 metres long and can carry 2,025 passengers (approximately).

2. The interior of the *QE2* is vast and the decor is similar to a modern hotel.

3. The beautiful winter garden on board the French passenger ship *Normandie*. She was launched in 1932 and was the world's largest ship when she entered service.

4. The smoking room of the *Queen Mary*. This liner, launched in 1934, was elegantly decorated in the most modern style of the day. The passengers played cards or simply relaxed in this room.

5. Deck games played in the shadow of one of the huge funnels of the *Queen Mary*. Sports and games were an important part of the leisure activities on every voyage.

6. On board the *Queen Mary* the decor, food, tableware and waiter service were of the highest standard. The passengers paid highly and expected a good service in return.

Warships of the two World Wars

The Napoleonic Wars at the beginning of the 19th century were followed by almost a hundred years of peace at sea interrupted only by minor naval conflicts, except for the short Russo-Japanese War (1905). During the 20th century the changes in naval warfare were greater than during the whole of previous naval history. Sail was replaced by steam. Smooth-bore, muzzle-loading, cannonball guns were replaced by breech-loading, explosive-shell, and long-range, accurate guns. Wood for ship-building was replaced by steel. Torpedoes, mines, radio communication, submarines and aircraft had also appeared. The only common link with the past was the problem of how to cope with the conflicting requirements of fire power and speed.

When the British battleship *Dreadnought* was launched in 1906 she outclassed everything afloat. She had ten massively powerful 12 inch long range guns and secondary armament of twenty-four 3-inch guns for repelling small, fast ships. By 1914 Britain had 24 ships of this class and Germany had 16. The only major fleet action of World War I was the Battle of Jutland in 1916 which had no outright victor but Britain remained the master of the sea.

The lesser classes of ships were the powerful battle-cruisers, the heavy and light cruisers and the destroyers. There were many specialized small vessels such as torpedo-boats, mine-layers, mine-sweepers and armed merchantmen. The merchant ships were used as convoy escorts or as decoy-ships for anti-submarine warfare. Germany also used merchant ships as surface raiders.

At the start of World War I the naval authorities began to realize the possibilities of using strange new flying machines for observation or attack. Before the end of the war in 1918 some cruisers had their upper decks cleared of obstructions and transformed into sea-going airfields. The aircraft carrier had appeared but it was still only a minor naval weapon.

The aircraft carrier became the strategic naval weapon of World War II from 1939 to 1945. New and more powerful battleships were built but these were easy targets for air attacks. The sinking of the Bismarck was largely helped by planes from the aircraft carriers HMS *Victorious* and *Ark Royal*. The small escort-carriers, developed as convoy escorts for aerial spotting and submarine attacks, were largely responsible for foiling the German U-boat offensive.

The importance of the aircraft carrier mainly became apparent in the battle in the Pacific. Fortunately for the American navy their six aircraft carriers were at sea when the rest of their Pacific fleet was raided on 7 December 1941 at Pearl Harbor in Hawaii. The big Pacific battles were decided by the aircraft carriers and the Japanese lost their carriers and their huge battleships to superior American, carrier-launched, air attacks.

◄ The destruction of American ships at Pearl Harbor was effective because the Japanese bomber pilots had carefully studied models and maps and practised continuously.

▼ The surprise attack on Pearl Harbor, Hawaii, on 7 December 1941, crippled the U.S. Pacific fleet. This dramatic picture shows three battleships hit from the air.

◄ The Battle of Jutland in 1916 was the major fleet action of World War I. Although the British sustained heavier casualties than the Germans they won the battle insofar as the German fleet retreated and did not put to sea again.

▼ The aircraft carrier HMS Ark Royal and her Swordfish fighters were part of Force H based in Gibraltar. It was her aircraft that crippled the Bismarck. Ark Royal was torpedoed in November 1941 by a submarine.

The threat beneath the waves

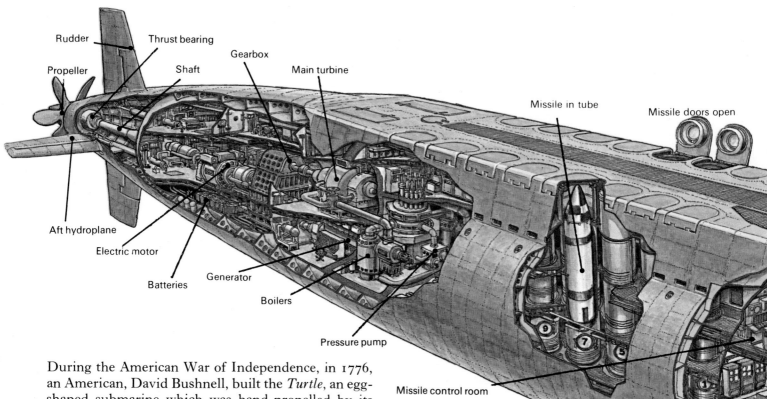

Rudder
Thrust bearing
Gearbox
Main turbine
Propeller
Shaft
Missile in tube
Missile doors open
Aft hydroplane
Electric motor
Batteries
Generator
Boilers
Pressure pump
Missile control room
Navigation room
Gyroscope
9
7
5

During the American War of Independence, in 1776, an American, David Bushnell, built the *Turtle*, an egg-shaped submarine which was hand-propelled by its one-man crew. This submarine reached the 64-gun HMS *Eagle* but failed to attach a mine to her. It escaped despite being spotted and pursued by a longboat.

In 1803 the American Robert Fulton built his hand-propelled *Nautilus* for Napoleon Bonaparte, and it successfully blew up a practice targetship. Bonaparte was not interested in this underwater ship nor was the British Admiralty when Fulton approached them with his idea. The first ship to be sunk by a submersible was the American Federal Navy's *Housatonic*, in 1864, by the Confederate submarine *H. L.* Hunley—which was also sunk by the explosion of its own mine. This showed, however, the possibilities of the submarine despite the difficulties of hand propulsion.

Combustion engines consumed far too much oxygen to be of any use under water. This problem was overcome by the introduction of electric motors running off batteries. The first modern submarine was the USS *Holland* built in 1900. It had a petrol engine for surface cruising and charging the batteries (for the electric motor used during dives) and it had a torpedo tube.

The real start of submarine warfare was in World War I when Germany used her submarines to sink enemy warships and merchant ships. This disrupted the flow of important goods to Britain and France. Britain, which started the war with a similar number of submarines to Germany, was not as successful because there were fewer German ships out at sea to act as targets. Germany could have done more harm to British shipping had she had more submarines.

▲ A 'composite' cut-away picture of a Royal Navy nuclear submarine incorporating features of several types. The main armament consists of strategic nuclear missiles and there are also torpedoes.

▼ An early submarine of French design: the Goubet biplace of 1889, adopted by the Imperial Russian Navy. It had a jointed screw, an electric motor and oars. The electric storage batteries can be seen forward.

▲ The nuclear powered submarine uses the heat generated in the uranium reactor core to produce steam for steam-turbines and for turbo-generators to provide vast electrical power.

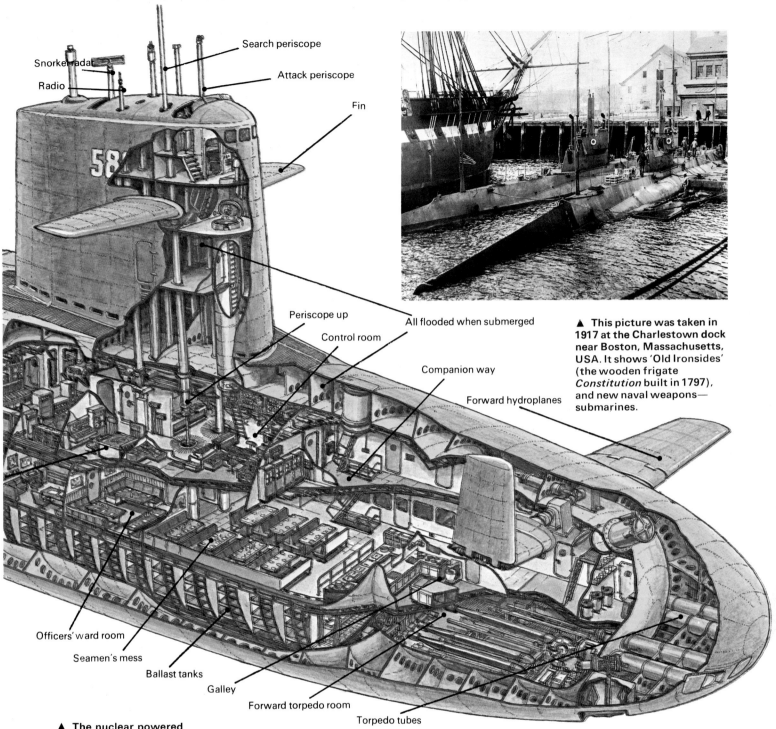

Snorkel radar

Radio

Search periscope

Attack periscope

Fin

581

Periscope up

Control room

All flooded when submerged

Companion way

Forward hydroplanes

Officers' ward room

Seamen's mess

Ballast tanks

Galley

Forward torpedo room

Torpedo tubes

▲ This picture was taken in 1917 at the Charlestown dock near Boston, Massachusetts, USA. It shows 'Old Ironsides' (the wooden frigate *Constitution* built in 1797), and new naval weapons—submarines.

▲ The nuclear powered submarines used by the British Navy carry 16 nuclear missiles. Once at sea the submarines cannot easily be traced by the enemy. They have almost unlimited endurance and do not rely on shore bases. The air purification system means that the submarine does not need to surface for air.

The nuclear reactor needs refuelling every five years. There is spacious accommodation for the crew of 144 men. There are two crews, one crew goes on patrol while the other is training or on leave.

World War II saw the introduction of the snorkel (an air-intake tube allowing the diesel engines and generator to be run while cruising just below the surface) and of sonar for submarine detection. World War II submarines were basically similar to those of World War I, but with many improvements.

The introduction of nuclear power in 1955 completely changed submarine warfare. Nuclear submarines can stay submerged for months on end because they carry an air purification system. They have a virtually unlimited range. In 1958 the USS *Nautilus* sailed under the ice pack to the North Pole and in 1960 the USS *Triton* sailed round the world without surfacing.

The new nuclear submarines can travel faster than 30 knots and can dive very deep. They are either 'hunters'—armed only with torpedoes for destroying enemy submarines or ships—or are strategic missile carriers, such as the U.S. Trident class ships which have nuclear missiles. These can be fired from under water to land targets up to 9,500 kilometres away.

Ships of today

Technological progress since World War II has meant a huge increase in the size and capacity of modern shipping.

Modern ship-design is concentrated on ease of building and has eliminated almost completely the use of curved metal plates, bringing about the boxy squared look of many modern freighters. The time-consuming tank trials of scale models have been partly replaced by computer simulation. Computers can be used to modify the lines of a ship until the best compromise between ease of building and hydro-dynamic shape is achieved.

The computer can control the machines that cut out the full-size steel plates. Originally plates were riveted and later welding appeared in the years between the two World Wars. Since the end of World War II the all-welded construction has been widely used. Prefabricated whole hull sections and superstructures are assembled beforehand, complete with pipings and wirings, and dropped in place by cranes on the launching dock.

The coal-burning boiler producing steam for a piston engine is almost a thing of the past. Most small- and medium-sized craft are motorvessels, powered by diesel engines. Large vessels are powered by steam turbines, the steam being produced either by oil-fired boilers or by a nuclear reactor.

New heat-resistant metal alloys now also allow the

◄ **The Very Large Crude Carrier** *Texaco London* (British flag) commissioned in 1976. She is 270,000 tons deadweight. Length 344 metres; breadth 54 metres; depth 26 metres. Cargo is crude oil.

▲ **The short-sea ferry** *Prins de Nederlanden* which transports vehicles as well as passengers.

▲ **The cargo-liner** *Fian* at Gravesend which carries cargo of many shapes and sizes.

▼ **A British Rail hovercraft** about to 'land' on a concrete hard at Dover.

▼ **The hydrofoil** *Condor 2* on the Alderney passenger run. Notice how the hull is lifted by the foils.

use of gas turbines that work directly on hot combustion gases. Navigation has also been revolutionized. RDF (Radio Direction Finding), radar and Consol (a sophisticated RDF) date back from World War II. Instantaneous and continuous position fixing by radio waves is now provided by sophisticated electronic systems.

Satellite navigation, which is precise and requires a computer on board, was until recently confined to some warships and scientific expeditionary vessels but is now found on some merchant vessels. Satellites also provide weather pictures and these, as well as weather forecast charts, can be transmitted to ships at sea. Ships can be rerouted to avoid delay by adverse weather conditions. The ships' engine and steering controls are largely automated.

The biggest trade today is that of crude oil. Large tankers are cheaper to operate than smaller ones and VLCCs (Very Large Crude Carriers) can reach up to 600,000 tons deadweight. They are the biggest ships ever built.

Cargo handling in harbour is costly and streamlining has been provided by using standard-size containers. These can be filled with goods at the factory and opened only at final destination. The containers are transported by container-carriers. LASHs (Lighters Aboard SHip) and BACATS (Barges Aboard CATamaran) can load and unload containers and goods at small ports lacking in big docking facilities. Ro-Ro (Roll-on, Roll-off) ferries provide an extension of road traffic across narrow seas and fast hovercrafts and hydrofoils transport passengers at car speed.

Ships through the ages

Egyptian ship

Greek galley

Roman grainship

Viking ship

Cog

Carrack

Caravel

Galleon

Galley

Ship-of-the-line

Clipper

Barque

Steam paddle ship

Iron warship

Battleship of WW1   Dreadnought

Aircraft carrier of WW11

Container ship

Crude Oil Tanker

Liner   QE2

VLCC

0   30   60
Scale in metres

0   30   60   90   120
These ships are drawn to scale

0   30   60

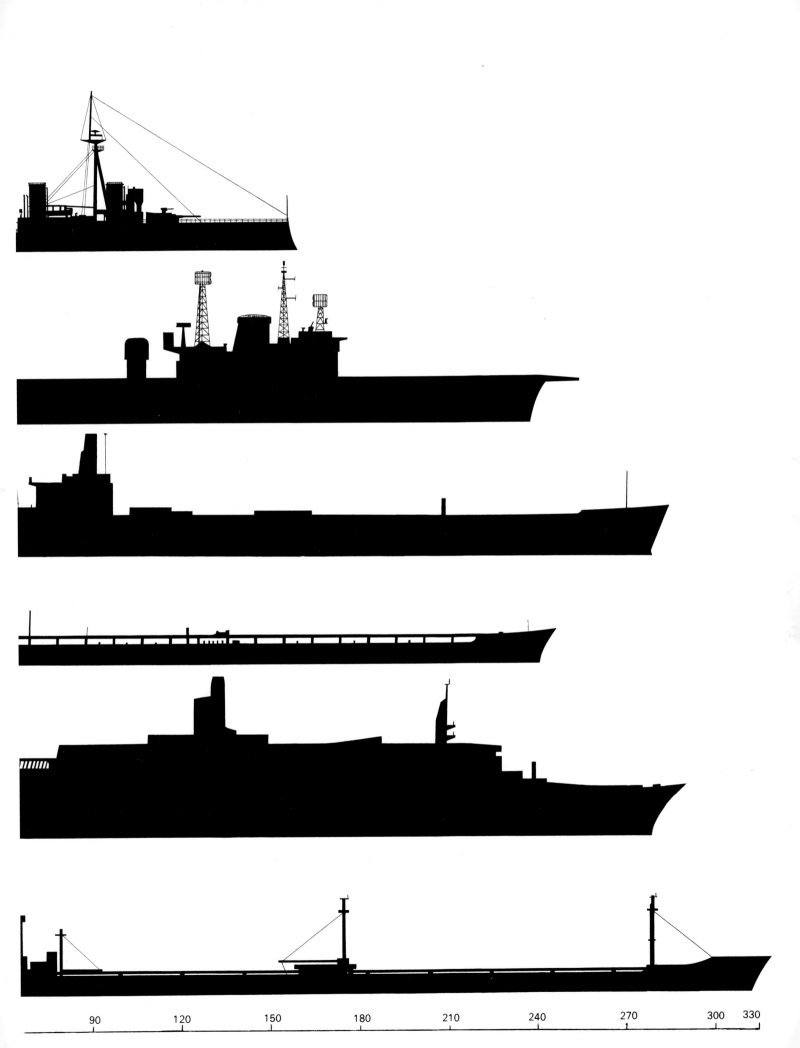

90 120 150 180 210 240 270 300 330

How to find out more

SAILING

Certainly the best way to get a better understanding of traditional sailing ships and to get a taste of what life aboard was like is to actually sail one! A number of former working sailing vessels continue to sail and earn a living by carrying passengers or trainees. They have retained their traditional rigs and they give a feeling of adventure and sense of history. There are also some modern purpose-built sail training vessels that have adopted some of the traditional looks of the genuine working craft.

CLUBS

Mariners International, 58 Woodville Road, New Barnet, Herts, is an international 'tall ship' club where, amongst other activities, members organize traditional ship cruises on a variety of rigs. Cruises are mixed and most are training cruises where all participants share in the working of the ship.

The Island Cruising Club, the Island, Salcombe, South Devon, operates a large dinghy fleet and several modern yachts and organizes cruises on the Brixham trawler *Provident*.

The *Thames Barge Sailing Club*, National Maritime Museum, Greenwich, London SE10, maintains and sails the sailing barges *Pudge* and *Centaur*.

The *International Sailing Craft Association* (ISCA), The Quay, Exeter, Devon, not only runs the Exeter Maritime Museum but also sails several of the Museum's unusual craft on the Exe or at sea.

The *Sail Training Association*, Bosham, Chichester, Sussex, operates two large purpose-built 3-masted topsail schooners *Sir Winston Churchill* and *Malcolm Miller*.

The *Sea Cadet Corps*, Offshore Command, HMS Dolphin, Gosport, Hants, operates a steel brig and a small yacht-brigantine for Sea Cadets and Girls' Nautical Training Corps members.

The *Irish Sail Training Association*, the Ministry of Defence, Parkgate St, Dublin 8, is currently building a wooden training brigantine.

MUSEUM SHIPS

These are old preserved vessels that do not sail any more but which are open to the public.

The clipper *Cutty Sark* is preserved and beautifully restored at Greenwich, London. The living accommodation is restored to its original appearance. There is also a collection of objects relating to the ship and to the clipper era and a large figurehead collection can be visited in the hold.

St Katharine's Dock, by the Tower of London, has a number of historical vessels open to the public. This dock is also a marina where one can usually see a large number of privately-owned Thames barges and some visiting gaff-riggers and schooners.

Near St Katharine's Dock, and on the opposite bank of the River Thames, one can visit the World War II cruiser HMS *Belfast*.

The First-rate ship-of-the-line HMS *Victory*, Nelson's flagship at the battle of Trafalgar, is preserved at HM Dockyard, Portsmouth, Hants. She is fully restored to her 1805 appearance.

At Brixham, S. Devon, one can visit a 'replica' of Drake's *Golden Hind*. She was built on the hull of a modern boat and gives an impression of what the small late 16th century galleons looked like.

The *ISCA Maritime Museum* at Exeter has the best collection in the world of preserved small and medium sized craft. The museum currently has more than 80 vessels including the world's oldest working steamboat, a dredger, dhows, Portuguese boats of several types and African dugouts.

Brunel's SS *Great Britain*, once the largest iron-built ship in the world, is being preserved and restored at the dock where she was built at Bristol. The first steam turbine vessel, the *Turbinia*, built in 1897, is preserved at the Museum of Science and Engineering at Newcastle-upon-Tyne.

The *Unicorn* is a 46-gun frigate which was laid down in 1794 and completed in 1824 and which is now an unmasted hulk at Victoria Dock, Dundee.

Modern ships, still working, can be seen in all ports but unfortunately the docks are sometimes enclosed by walls or fences and closed to the public. When naval ships (Royal Navy or guests from abroad) call into a civilian port they often have open days when they allow visitors on board.

MUSEUMS

The *National Maritime Museum* at Greenwich, London, is undoubtedly the best of its kind in the world. Its exhibits cover the whole span of maritime history. Temporary exhibitions on a particular theme are frequently organized, as well as lectures and film shows.

The *Science Museum* in South Kensington, London, has a collection of ship models and navigational objects.

The *Victory Museum* is located by HMS *Victory* at Portsmouth and has good exhibits about Nelson and the Battle of Trafalgar.

The *City of Liverpool Museum*, William Brown St, Liverpool, has a collection concerning commercial shipping, with models of fishing and coastal vessels.

The *Maritime Museum of Kingston-on-the-Hull*, Pickering Park, Kingston-on-the-Hull, covers mainly the rich local maritime history, including whaling and trawling.

The *Royal Scottish Museum*, Chambers St, Edinburgh, includes extensive maritime exhibits, ship models, working engine models, etc.

The *Museum of Transport*, Glasgow, has a very large collection of ship models exhibited in its Department of Technology, with photographs and drawings.

BOOKS

The Ship by Björn Langström (Allen and Unwin)
The Lore of Ships by Tre Trickare (Crescent Books, New York)
The Adventure of Ships (Hamlyn)
Sailing Ships by Patrick Brophy (Hamlyn)
Ships of the High Seas by Erik Abranson (Peter Lowe)
The Age of Exploration by John R. Hales and Others (Time-Life Books)
Pirates by David Mitchell (Thames and Hudson)
Pirates and Buccaneers by John Gilbert (Hamlyn)
Nelson's Navy by Roger Hart (Wayland)
Sea Life in Nelson's Time by John Masefield (Sphere Books)
Sailors of the Great Sailing Ships by Erik Abranson (Macdonald Educational)
Two Years Before the Mast by Richard Henry Dana (Dent)
The Cruise of the Cachalot by Frank Bullen (Murray)

Index